DUTCH STORIES

OF HIS MOST FAMOUS REGION

BY

JAN PRINS

COLOPHON

www.janprins.com

This book is pure fiction, it falls in the so named faction genre. This fictitious events mixed and displayed against and in a historical context.

To the extent that the events described the reality this approach is based on mere coincidence and has this does not pretend to describe the reality or the purpose and/or to display.

All persons in this book are borne by the author. Some similarities with existing -died or surviving- persons is based on pure chance.

Colophon:
Press: first edition, October 2016 (reprint of The Thinker Tells)

Publisher: Jan Prins
© 2016 Jan Prins (Standard Copyright License)
    www.janprins.com
Coverphoto: J. Prins

ISBN/EAN: 978-1539696698
NUR: 301

All events and persons

are imaginary.

TABLE OF CONTENTS:

ABOUT THE BOOK

Everything is ordinary to us until we get know its history. We start to see things differently when we do get a glimpse of its past.

The Netherlands has many beautiful areas and prominent places, but if there is a region that really catches the eye, it is the Gooi. This place started to be popular because of the famous TV series in Netherlands, "Gooische Vrouwen" (Gooi Women).

In this book, you will get to know the Gooi in a different way. This book covers the topics about credit crisis, retirees, and much more about the Gooi.

This book will take you on a trip to the Gooi in a way of having fact and fiction intertwined. Do not take everything that's on here literally, because the author has such vivid imagination!

FOREWORD

Everything is ordinary to us until we get know its history. We start to see things differently when we do get a glimpse of its past.

The Netherlands has many beautiful areas and prominent places, but if there is a region that really catches the eye, it is the Gooi. This place started to be popular because of the famous TV series in Netherlands, "Gooische Vrouwen" (Gooi Women).

In this book, you will get to know the Gooi in a different way. This book covers the topics about credit crisis, retirees, and much more about the Gooi.

This book will take you on a trip to the Gooi in a way of having fact and fiction intertwined. Do not take everything that's on here literally, because the author has such vivid imagination!

The stories in this book are a selection of the most successful ones that have appeared in a blog and some previous publications.

I hope you have a lot of fun with this book!

THE GOOI

The Gooi is found in the south-eastern corner of the province of North Holland in the Netherlands. Aside from the background of the Gooi, you will also find the reflections of a resident, who was astounded by a wide range of issues in this book.

The history is clear that the Gooi always had a certain appeal.

Important trade routes ran through that area; there was beautiful nature and infrastructure.

Wealthy merchants settled in the Gooi. It has become the place of radio and television.

In Hilversum, a Philips factory was established, as well as a radio school. Because of that, a lot of broadcasting studios emerged on that place.

The first TV broadcast took place in a studio in Bussum named **Irene.**

Your writer has seen this studio burn down twice!

First, as a child; standing on the playground, I saw the smoke rising high.

Years later, I saw the reporter Harmen Siezen on the news with an apologetic look saying he unfortunately had to demolish the place as the studio was burning on the background.

With the housing of all known radio and television personalities, there came the tabloid, and also the notion of the **Gooi Mattress**.

Now, after many years, Linda de Mol with her **Gooi Women** ensures that you will get to read positive and negative things about the Gooi in this book.

*

But back to the beginning: The Gooi arose during the Ice Period. Due to the shifting of large ice, big hills and moors were formed.

In the **Geological Museum** in Laren, it is easy to see how that took place. The Gooi was more or less a mound. The upland the Gooi is one of the oldest inhabited regions of the Netherlands.

It is a very interesting area with many interesting and historical places at the same time.

The city of Naarden is an ancient fortress. It was originally an old fishing village. The places Bussum, Laren and Blaricum were originally old peasant villages. Hilversum is now a broadcasting city.

They were built around waterholes for livestock; mainly sheep were kept. **The Gooische Erfgooiers** provided such a rich history.

As mentioned earlier, the Gooi is in many ancient writings because of the trade route that ran from Germany to Amsterdam.

During the Golden Age, numerous tradesmen settled in the Gooi that is why it became a rich country. Many stately mansions are found there; proof that it was indeed a place for a lot of rich people. Even in times of war, the Gooi was visited by Napoleon.

In short, there was always a certain tension in the region, but the real impetus came by a remarkable coincidence: **The Gooische Tramway.**

*

Hotellier Jan Hamdorff owned the famous Laren Hotel. He was looking for ways to increase his sales, and so he came into contact with Cornelis Bok.

Together, they devised a plan to open up a tramway. It was started in 1880 and then in 1881, it was connected to Naarden.

In 1882, Hilversum was connected to Laren. Later, the line was extended from Naarden to Amsterdam. There was also a branch to Bussum and Muiderberg.

The stories about this tram are legendary: wherever they came, they left her traces; often in the form of many accidents. That was the reason that it was soon nicknamed The Killer of the Gooi.

The use of a steam locomotive was the reason that there are occasional thatched roofs that ignite the sparks from the pipe; **The Killer of the Gooi** left a bloody trail blazing.

The purpose of Jan Hamdorff was reached: Laren awakened from an ancient sleep and began a rapid development.

Not only was Laren discovered, but also the entire Gooi.

Day trippers fled the big city of Amsterdam and sought the peace and nature. Restaurants were heading for a golden age, and even the retail sector flourished.

Many people from Amsterdam came to the Gooi for a peaceful vacation.

Laren was very crowded because of the flow of tourists who were amazed at the rustic farms and scenic spots.

This was reinforced by the arrival of the painter Jozef Israels in 1874. He found the perfect place to do his work in peace and was inspired by the rustic houses and its inhabitants and surroundings. He urged his friends to follow his example and not much later, Laren was discovered as THE painting village.

Laren is known as an artists' village. Painters from the Netherlands, but also far beyond, discovered Laren as a unique, forgotten village.

It inspired generations of painters; innovative, traditional, poor, misunderstood; basically everyone who has painting as a hobby.

They all went there to exhibit their work. Anton Mauve was known for his paintings of herds of sheep in Laren. Those paintings were exported to the United States.

The American artist, William Singer, was inspired by this and came to live in Laren together with his wife. After his death in 1956, his wife founded the **Singer Memorial Foundation** in memory of her husband.

A venue for many artists was: "The Pub". This pub was demolished in 1979 to be a part of the hotel Hamdorff.

I often visited an exhibition in that place with my father, who was a painter.

The harpist Rosa Spier came up with the idea that the Gooi could be a "safe haven for older artists." In 1963, Henriette Polak founded the Rosa Spier Foundation. The intention was to build place for older artists to work in and have personal care. **The Rosa Spier House** opened in 1969.

*

But as I said, the cause of this development was the arrival of the Gooische Tramway that made it possible for fast travel from Amsterdam to the Gooi; especially to the popular Laren.

The drivers of the city were getting more concerned about the health status of the residents of Amsterdam, and they were also faced with a shortage of nursing, so they looked for possibilities of staying in the Gooi.

There was even talk of clean air, space, and peace and quiet. The result was the establishment of numerous health institutions, such as:

The Children hospital of the Trappenberg (now Rehabilitation)

Sanatorium Juliana Refuge (now addiction clinic Symphora)

High Laren Hospital and Sanatorium (now Hospital in the Gooi)

Student Sanatorium (now nursing house the Stichtse Hof

Sanatorium Sunburst (after hospital and nursing home now)

Asthma Center Heideheuvel

And many other smaller institutions.

In this way, the pressure on health care in Amsterdam was removed because there are literally hundreds of patients that were nursed in the Gooi.

Many jobs were created, and as a result, health institutions soon became a very large source of work. Moreover, they came to live in the Gooi in the many sister houses.

The visitors of these patients came with the Gooische Tramway, a fast and easy connection. Since then, buses came back and forth from Amsterdam to the Gooi.

A few years back, one could even travel to the middle of the Brink in Laren to Amsterdam.

*

That was the reason why more and more people discovered Laren; day trippers, visitors to the healthcare, and commuters; eventually, they came for the artists and shops.

With the advent of the car, it was of course always easier to leave the city behind and look in the picturesque village of Laren, with its many farms and entertaining places.

The connection to the big city, by chance, eventually became the lifeblood and the reason for the existence of Laren as we know today.

CRISIS

When I think of the current credit banks or land crisis, then the first thing I can think about is our former finance minister, Gerrit Zalm, by starting the Euro in 2002.

Oh poor man. Our minister had never been shopping and had no idea what a loaf of bread, let alone a carton of milk cost.

It took us at least 10% of our savings and pension funds by the wrong exchange he had agreed. Our pensioned people yielded the same rate, and because he was so naive not to use the Prices Act, we were faced with a perceived inflation, which continues rumbling.

Recently, there was a picture of the same Gerrit Zalm, chairman of ABN-Amro Bank, with Boele Staal, President of the Bank Club, in all the papers. They were sweeping the tears from their eyes as they laugh at all those people that they fooled.

What was going on? They were heard by the Second Chamber of the Parliament on bank bonuses.

"This must continue," they shouted in unison. The entire banking sector was found to have the last credit and banking

crisis. They were really stubborn and contempt for their customers. Shame!

Because of just selling opaque as the profiteering and letting go clear of their main competitor, the DSB Bank went bankrupt. They had an immense harm to the entire Dutch population; the lock housing, building on his back, the pension issues, and so on.

Our confidence in politics is thoroughly drilled into the ground. The controls of the Dutch Central Bank and the Financial Markets Authority appeared totally out of date and inadequate.

The arrogance of Wellink did horrify us. What a man!

Politicians had it inspected and were left with the debris.

Fortunately, the policy had a room for them in the real world.

Our leaders of yesteryear were chief executive in the banking and consulting world.

Consider Wim Kok at ING. Think of Wouter Bos at KPMG and Jan Peter Balkenende at Moret & Young; they knew what was good for us!

They left us with a mess. They dropped their social masks and appeared to be the grabbers of the Big Money.

*

The common man is hit by one after the other measure, so they get much less mortgage, they do not earn too much to qualify for rental house banks, and give nothing for savings. The mortgage lending rates raised more questions around us.

The profits of the banks are growing like never before, and the bonuses are finding their way back.

Mr. Zalm and his associates just laugh. Deception gets a facial!

The cause of the crisis has been always there even before the introduction of the euro in the Netherlands. We all just become poorer.

Former President Bush stated that all citizens should be able to qualify to buy a house, even if they had no job. How stupid can you be!

These mortgages were sold as packages to investors and banks, so the case clapped as first.

It started with the Lehman Bank and now, we could, thanks to Wikileaks, read that 14 of the 15 banks in America are to collapse.

Fortunately, Obama came in as Bush's successor. But did the financial world learn its lessons? No, they just went back about their business and did not care about the control of President Obama.

*

The financial world is globalized, so the effects were felt in all countries, but especially in the Netherlands. It is because we have the largest investor in America and major global financial institutions.

Our banks and pension funds invest a lot of money in America that customers and participants are brought together.

It's easy to gamble with other people's money, because they themselves do not have to pay if it goes wrong with the bill. They gambled, they lost, and we are on the blisters.

Banks and pension funds have large investment departments with numerous experts. Therefore, it remains very strange that they just invest in this way. They even invest in the southern euro zone countries, those countries. We do not know where their deception came from, but we cannot let them go bankrupt, because yes, think about the investments that we have there!

So they had to be supported. The position of the strong euro countries also eroded.

Consider the fact that the Netherlands only has a good pension system in Europe.

Now that we all get less or no mortgage, they are even planning a redemption of 50% mandatory! So yes, we get lesser pension, because of these investments!

Today, car dealers and brokers are more familiar than bankers. Jesus called his disciples in the early Christian times to drive, because of their deceit of the common people. Our bankers are the tax collectors of this time. They are the robber chieftains!

It's strange that I recently read about the village Blaricum. The most expensive place in the Netherlands, where home sales by as much as 59% increase in one year and the prices by 12%. It took an average of € 788,688 for a house! Laren's sales increased by as much as 85%, but priced with "only" 1%. The average price was € 609,967.

That is different than the nationwide declines and prices that we see elsewhere.

This made things abundantly immoral, since people on "top" still earn more, while John Doe struggles to live.

*

We see that in Tunisia and Egypt, the anger is focused on dictators who have been in power for decades. We read how the wife of President Ben Ali of Tunisia went off with gold reserves.

The family of President Mubarak of Egypt fled to London with 100 cases in their possession!

We read how the Mubarak family has years of money transferred abroad, numerous investments, homes, airplanes, etc.

All the major companies in Egypt were a relative of the Mubarak's in position, and half of the annual profits had to be relinquished.

All foreign investors were required an Egyptian "partner" who should have 51% of the shares needed and therefore, profits.

It is estimated that Egypt has spent a total of between 25 to 100 billion dollars.

The land is left destitute and many countries around suffer the same thing.

Let us be careful. In the Netherlands, the gap between rich and poor is never increased.

We see what people are able to do!

SIGNS OF TIME

We live in a rapidly changing time. The digital revolution is increasingly becoming revolutionary in the real world.

Wael Ghonim of Google in Egypt has said, via his Facebook page, that a revolution in the country actually had that effect.

He was inspired to do so by the same movement, just a week before, in Tunisia.

The result was that, President Ben Ali of Tunisia fled the country.

His wife was even faster, and she took a very large part of the gold reserves with her!

Egypt President, Mubarak, first announced to never step down after the elections, but a week later, he resigned. A transition to a new constitution and new elections are put in motion.

Within ten days, his regimen of 32 years was done!

The wave of Facebook calls for change went to Yemen, Jordan, and it goes on like a tidal wave through the Middle East.

What is going on here? What the hell happened here?

The Internet is widely used by everyone. A lot of people became aware of the situation in the governments all over the world. It made the control of communication within the press somewhat impossible. Censorship became hard to do. We can look up any information with Google and to us, the whole world is just on our screens.

Cell phones were introduced in cautious ways, but gradually, it became everyone's possession.

Then the social websites like YouTube, Myspace, LinkedIn, Twitter, and especially Facebook came.

This is a fast, very fast, communication with citizens of all levels of difficulty, not only within the country, but even globally.

First, it was only possible through the computer, but now, even mobile phones are capable of doing anything.

Moreover, it was not only for calls, but also for SMS (by the way, invented by a Dutchman).

On Blogs and forums on the Internet, many express their opinions and comments about certain issues.

In short, everyone and everything is accessible directly without wasting time and information.

The youth manifest the Internet in many ways, and often used it to communicate with one another.

And then came WikiLeaks.

The Australian hacker, Assange, showed his people all the information within and between Governments and the Internet.

And guess what? We all feel that we were fooled by the governments and public administrations on a massive scale. Even the negotiations between Israel and the Palestinians proved to be a farce.

Suddenly it became clear that 14 of the 15 banks in America were to collapse during the banking crisis.

The diplomatic services in all U.S. embassies proved that there were true spies nests for all personal details of every citizen and was passed on to Washington.

And at the time of writing, there is only a small part of the WikiLeaks documents released, who knows what awaits us.

The reaction:

That was inevitable.

Awakened by WikiLeaks, many citizens felt like they had enough.

Citizens demanded clarity and stopping global deception.

Organized democracy turned out not to be able to comment on the problems and issues of our time, let alone within the dictatorial regimes in the world.

It was therefore logical that the turmoil first hit.

They had plenty of poverty, unemployment, and enrichment of the summit.

And so it was seized to Facebook; people were called via their mobile phones to take action and to revolt.

Signs of time:

It is not enough to be able to cast your vote in the four years since the gap between citizens and the government only seems to be widening.

Three quarters of the Dutch population do not want a military transmission to Afghanistan, but it turns out we do, thanks to Jolande Sap, anyway.

Is that the democracy that we have in mind? NO!

The Netherlands is not Egypt, but let's beware that in no time, an organization can arise.

That can come from all sides, even from politics. The Twitter messages from politicians like Geert Wilders and Femke Halsema are followed a lot.

Minister of Foreign Affairs, Uri Rosenthal, makes a decision and a tweet from Geert makes him ridiculous.

We are formation a government, hop a tweet from Femke, and then we know what it stands for.

And so everyone can be critically monitored, and therefore, one is forced to take into account the opinions and demands of the citizens; the citizens they represented in politics.

Politics should be borne by the citizens. It should not manipulate its citizens.

Quote of the newspaper Vrij Nederland of February 9, 2011:

The Egyptian revolution gets a face:

Who will be the face of the Egyptian revolution? The 30 year old Wael Ghonim has a good chance. Ghonim was arrested two weeks ago by the Egyptian secret police and was held in a secret place. Two days ago, he was released. In Tahrir Square, he spoke briefly in a frenzied crowd. The reason why there were so many people was because of a very emotional interview from Ghonim immediately after his release on the private channel "Dream TV".

In the interview, the 30-year-old marketing director of Google for the Middle East admitted that he was the anonymous 'administrator' behind the Facebook page calling for demonstrations against the regime. He also has a twitter account: @Ghonim. The youthful Facebook supporters formed the basis for what is now the White Revolution in Egypt. It was also called the # 25jan-revolution.

Ghonim, who looked very tired during the interview, repeatedly broke into tears. He said: "I'm not a hero, but the people on the streets who are being beaten up are. I'm just someone who is sitting behind a computer and my keyboard." He began to grumble that he was pick up from the streets and detained without informing his family. "There is no one who leads the masses. This revolution belongs to the Internet youth. The revolution belongs to everyone in Egypt. I love my country."

"It is not time to negotiate," Ghonim said to his supporters in the square. "Egypt above all!"

Ghonim disappeared after his performance at the Tahrir Square in the crowd. "I'm very tired," he finally said, and disappeared into the crowd. We will hear more from him.

End of quote.

RETIREMENT

There is nothing greater than to retire after a lifelong work. The former Prime Minister Daddy Drees decided that on the 65th birthday, men will finally stop with working and retire.

Back then, you would be happy to retire earlier than 65 years. But because of the hardships in the economy, people must work longer.

It so happened that in 2011 will be the 65th anniversary of the end of the Second World War. It was extensively celebrated with great sexual activity with or without our liberators. There was a real Baby boom.

"The hippies retire," screams a headline.

All kinds of famous people turn out to be retired by 65 years of age; Guus Hiddink, Adriaan van Dis, Paul Witteman, Bennie Jolink, and many others. *"Finally I'll get a steady income,"* sighed Jules Deelder.

In 2011, there will be 231,500 people that will retire versus 167,000 in the previous year. It increased by 40%.

As a result, 645,000 additional people will be withdrawn from the labor market, so the numbers of the unemployed, disabled, and benefit claimants will fall sharply.

The demand for labor will be larger, and therefore it is hoped that the new Dutch minister would finally come up with the labor market to fill that gap.

Such a problem is solved again.

Everyone was happy, you might think.

But no, envy sticks his head up.

Suddenly there is a strong current, which emerges in various publications. The boomers like a bunch of exploiters who have enriched the grabbers, have the Slochteren gas field and robbed them good.

*

Recently, there was a picture of the same Gerrit Zalm, chairman of ABN-Amro Bank, with Boele Staal, President of the Bank Club, in all the papers. They were sweeping the tears from their eyes as they laugh at all those people that they fooled.

What was going on? They were heard by the Second Chamber of the Parliament on bank bonuses.

"This must go on," they shouted in unison. The entire banking sector was found to have the last credit and banking crisis. They were really stubborn and had contempt for their customers. Shame!

The DSB Bank went bankrupt. They caused immense harm to the entire Dutch population; the lock housing, building on his back, the pension issues, and so on.

It was very strange that at the time of retirement of the Baby Boom generation, it seemed that all financial products were unsound. The pension funds were actually unable to return from retirement in the normal way. The youth were blamed. They assumed that they were not being awarded. The insurance they have paid for was not returned to them. What's behind it?

The government has covered a nice trick from former Prime Minister Ruud Lubbers.

They had so much money that they no longer knew and even premium was greatly reduced because they were actually not needed. But then they had a premium deficiency, but because there is no salary space, it means a loss of income for the people.

They invested in lucrative holiday parks in France, in shopping malls in America and so on. We were the largest investor in America, but we seemed to have failed to invest in our own economy!

Nothing too crazy.

And suddenly, in 2009, they came up with the funds with a calculation that was unfavorable. This has always been based on a three year average, but suddenly had to be based on the daily exchange rate.

The results were: things collapsed and payment out the pension funds were frozen and even decreased in some cases.

They additionally found out after that occurrence that we were all older than before. How clever of them!

Even the auditors and actuaries do not trust the pension funds that they themselves controlled for years.

Is that a coincidence?

Of course not. For years, they have happily used our deposited funds; they have bonuses, but they forgot that they once had to pay.

"Think of a list, Tom Poes", would have exclaimed Mr. Bommel.

And they are the reason of the sorrow of four million retired people. SHAME!

*

But what is the reality?

The reality is that after World War II, our parents have worked to give their children a better future.

The country was rebuilt and people slowly scribbled.

My mother washed our only night suit and hoped that on the evening it was dry so it could be used again.

My mother sat hunched over the knitting machine; in an attempt to save money.

I can still see myself standing on the shoreline with my two brothers, dressed in the same knitted swimsuit.

We were embarrassed by the fact that our swimwear just looked too old and just do not fit us well.

Wednesday afternoon, we went to the house of our domestic help, who had TV.

It was black and white, but you could still watch Ivanhoe or watch news being announced by an announcer.

We were squeezing ourselves in the room with all the children in the neighborhood.

Those were the times. It was different from Twitter or Facebook and YouTube.

The emotion in the assassination of President Kennedy was something to never be forgotten!

His funeral and his son who saluted would forever be burned on your retina; that image will never leave you.

We were happy and our parents stopped their funds in pension funds and paid tax in the sacred belief that we would benefit from it. We did not know the conspiracy that the government had back then.

What a joy to drive that car on Dutch soil, the Daffodil.

We drove no faster than 110 km / h, but still, we drove.

We had that boyish pleasure in scouting, quests, campfires, the bridges, and so on.

It was memorable and has shaped us into who we are today.

Oh, there are so many more memories: the need to create coal, the allotment that we had kept for the homegrown vegetables, decorating houses to still get the holiday feeling, and so on.

The whole time, we were thinking that our contribution would be in a good state pension fund and give us a nice retirement! How did they ever get us to believe?

*

Despite everything, we retire.

We all looked forward to finally being able to travel, make cruises, do nice things for our wives, and needed nothing more.

But we seemed to have forgotten about something: the Wife!

She was horrified by the thought of her love to have all those freedom!

That could not and that was not allowed by her.

The man thus became an exile in his own house. When a friend of the wife came, he had to scram to his study, to the attic, just wherever, as longs as he gets to hide.

There is even a case in which the woman have seen a special room, complete with bed, what her husband has arranged for his collection of tin soldiers. He placed them there to reenact famous battles to be away from her.

Many women shudder at the thought of their man being at the house the whole day.

Some women are more tactical and made it easier for their spouse to enjoy their retirement by subscribing them to the Golf course and making them take lessons with a professional.

The romance of the first was long gone, and they just wanted to preserve their freedom at any cost.

You see a lot of lonely cyclists slowly pull through the landscape and the retired men who are sent to the street. It has also become increasingly busy on the golf courses. A lot of old men came there.

Yes, sometimes you see a couple in the streets; the man with a hollow and empty look, behind his well-dressed wife, and pain with his credit card.

There are, thankfully, exceptions. Happy couples who live together as buddies and go through life. They enjoy what life offers to them: vacations, grandchildren, etc.

But anyway, through the retirement of the Baby Boom Generation, our society will change completely. It will be interesting times.

So we go to the end with King Parkinson's and Queen Alzheimer's!

NOTE 1:

Today we read in:

TELEGRAPH, 05 Feb 2011, 13:12

"Pension funds miss out 145 billion Euro"

AMSTERDAM – has performed poorly in comparison with other investors in Europe over the last 20 years. In total, institutional investors had collected 145 billion Euros. They were able to get about 20,000 Euros per participant. This section calculates the television broadcast of the Zembla Saturday.

"If this had been private investment, then you had set your asset to the side and made use of it for a long time." said Ewald Engelen, Professor of Financial Geography at the University of Amsterdam. "But that could not be done by the Dutch employees, because they are required to participate in the
38

pension funds. "Pension funds were invested in more and more shares since the nineties. Because of the two stock market crises in 2002 and 2008, the funds significantly eroded, says Zembla. The Dutch Central Bank concluded in 2009 that the funds lost 112 billion by the stock market crash a year earlier. I was involved with that business, and the government also took billions out of the funds of the pension funds. If this had not taken place, this reduction would have been lower, according to the analysis of Zembla. There would now be 799 billion in pension funds, more than doubling the current reserves. The coverage ratio, which indicates whether pension funds are sufficient to fulfill their obligations to compliance, would have been 240 percent. That would have been more than enough to offset the increased life expectancy, inflation and financial setbacks, concludes Zembla."

End of quote

CONCLUSION:

The Dutch Polder Model appears, in this case, the bankrupt for the retiree.

The management of the pension retirement funds usually consists of a mix of representatives of workers, employers, and the Government. The association often decides whether the pension money is be to use for salary or structural improvements in the wage model.

In addition, employers had to reduce operating expenses even if there was more than enough.

The pension fund failed and was not applied.

All funds from the deferred wages of workers (the official word for pension) were abused for short-term goals at the expense of future retirees.

Now, you might think that all of that was because of the Gooi.

Laren, for example, has the greatest retiree population in the Netherlands. The rest of the scramble is under the minimum pension income and still has the possibility to decline.

The spending and should go down.

We see very clearly in this region that first signs are already there.

NOTE 2

Shortly after my comments about the pension retirement funds and the baby boomers, I had the pleasure to receive an invitation for a meeting of retired people in the building of the Pension Retirement Health and Welfare Fund in Zeist.

It had been years since I had been there. It was such a familiar territory. I was amazed at the empty parking lots and dead-looking and empty buildings.

Wandering around, I clung to a construction worker who explained to me that I had go around the corner to get to the new entrance. I did and I saw a brand new building with a large basement garage. It was no wonder there was not a car in sight.

I reported to the front desk and got a badge in connection with the monitoring. Moments later, I was too stunned to see 10 modernized meeting rooms equipped with the latest electronics. So it was there that the pension money went!

Our meeting was in a theater that many directors would envy.

One of the speakers was a board member of the pension fund. He was explaining how precarious the situation is and that further interventions would not be excluded. He was shameless as he spoke. He was sensing how he made a fool of himself.

It was just too pathetic to even ask a question.

While they are all bathed in luxury and huge salaries, the common man is squeezed. For years, there is no question of indexing, and that will just go on. Maybe the pensions will be reduced, but one thing is certain: it will not hurt them!

I remember the risky investments in shopping centers in America and holiday parks in France. I thought about why they didn't just invest the pension fund for the healthcare salaries.

It was just so crazy that they had so much money that they did not know what to do with it. It is sad, because the answer is obvious. They did not do what seemed right, and now the common people would not see what they hoped and expected.

GOOI WOMAN

As we have seen, Laren has become really popular.

There was initially a lot of attention from day-trippers and tourists. The population n of women who were attracted to quaint shops also increased.

Laren became quite a **fashion village**.

Typical stores are not there. If you're looking for a computer magazine, then you better just go somewhere else.

Laren became quite a place for women. It is where mothers and daughters go where they use their husbands and fathers' credit cards.

The fashion shows are well attended and once a year, there is a mega show on the Brink (a village green) where it is presented on a deck above the pond. Beautiful models show off the new winter collections.

Crowds of people came for that in Laren that is why the streets are always full of eye-pleasing women that are perfectly dressed in the latest fashions and walking in the most beautiful boots. They all looked very conscious with their appearances. They all want to be seen.

The men are usually provocative and mischievous. Laren is a place filled with real women, and the men are proud of their wives and they have to offer.

The mobile phone is an indispensable tool to make contact and that suits them.

*

Shopping is very tiring, but fortunately, there are a lot if restaurants and terraces where one can rest and have their lunch. Lunch is to be the most sought after in **Aùbere**. **Mauve** is always full and the **Prinsemarij** (former Police station) is always crowded.

If you go to those restaurants, you would walk in a really quiet place. You will get to see a lot of women drinking their wines and not speaking with each other or even make calls. No seat would be unoccupied, but fortunately, there is the famous Café called **het Bonte Paard** (Spotted Horse). It is where you can quietly grab a beer on the terrace and have a cigar while watching the **Coeswaerde**, the pond on the Brink.

There are a lot of car-spotters, young boys armed with cameras to capture photos of expensive cars like Jaguars, Roll Royce's, Bentleys, and so on. Those cars most likely have fast guys behind the wheel and are probably accompanied by highly bleached blonde beauties.

All of that is a rewarding project for them. They put those photos on the web, as if it were their own property.

*

With all those women in Laren, Linda de Mol had an idea to write **Gooische Women**. It is a series that has been immensely popular.

It is certain that many divorces occur among the people of Laren and Blaricum; just as elsewhere. The cause is often because the young men are afraid to take paternal responsibilities.

They prefer to go out with friends, travel, and enjoy life by gaming. The desire to have children among the young Dutch men is the lowest in Europe, and they have a big fear of commitment. They prefer to stay long with their parents.

The result is that, most of the responsibilities are on the shoulders of the women and that is partly the cause of their independent attitude and behavior.

But there is also another cause of divorce; the large number of successful men who are exposed to the temptations of life. There are many who had second or third marriages. But because the Gooi is a place with well people, men who get divorce leave their ex-wives with wealth and nice houses. Sometimes, it is also because they also do feel responsible about things.

It is also why the Gooi is a place where women seek for new relationships.

However, these relationships are actually a perpetual motion, because who marries his mistress creates a vacancy.

*

Then there are also the so-called **Real Gooische Girls**: young girls driving around fast on scooters. They are beautiful, sporty, walking on Uggies, but often very stupid. Their parents take care of them well.

They weekly go to beauticians, to a personal trainer for their health and tight and lean body. In the shops and on the terraces, you can see them drink cocktails or wine if it were lemonade.

To see and be seen is their big game.

Money is no object, because **"It is better to be spoiled than neglected,"** is their motto.

They live in such beautiful homes.

Their sports are hockey, tennis, golf, and horse riding. Most important thing for them are parties. Real Gooi girls party hard.

There was time that I went past through two girls violently bickering if they had four or eight parents. They literally lost count. Poor girls.

*

If you really want to get an idea of the true meaning of fashion in Laren, I suggest you come to **Café het Bonte Paard** (Spotted Horse) around four in the afternoon.

You would see a lot of women looking gorgeous and expensive.

Moments later, you will also get to see their Land Rovers or BMWs filled with shopping bags. They are most probably on their way to their husbands.

How do they explain that? It's like that's their only duty as wives, and it never stops.

It's more likely that their husbands go home really late at night because they are with their secretaries or on a business trip.

That's why shopping gives them comfort. They are women trying to get away from loneliness.

HOMELESS

After wandering, enjoying the beautiful scenery and the surprising views in the Gooi, it is always good to have somewhere to rest in.

On the way I saw Grandpa and his granddaughter admiring a red and white mushroom. Other people basked in the sun and cyclists wandered through the countryside. Small children were playing in a sand drift, while their mothers are on a bench reading a newspaper.

I was sitting on the terrace of restaurant **De Goede Gooier** (the Good Gooi-men) and looked out over the moors of Blaricum.

A strange name actually. Who is it or what does it mean?

I thought back to the phenomenon of Woman of the Gooi. It was described in the previous chapter, but could the old owners of this restaurant have still not envisioned a new name?

Yes, the shopkeepers in Laren find this name as the most appropriate for them, for sure!

My mind wandered involuntarily and I returned to that village where I went a long time ago.

There was a lot that remained the same, but there was also a lot that has changed. It became busier and more varied.

The many fields, the endless hedge, many thatched roofs, and narrow winding streets give you the look of a distant past. It gives you a romantic feeling when you see all of it.

The village having the highest aging rate of land was not really noticeable.

That is because of the size of visitors, hundreds of thousands per year. They affect the impression that you will have on the place.

The streets in this place are surprisingly really different. I am talking about the traffic, or rather the lack of it.

On their discovery to the latest fashion, the ladies do not allow themselves to behave the way they should while driving.

Once they see something interesting across the street, they immediately just try to get there right away, without being cautious.

They drive like kamikaze pilots through the narrow streets which unfortunately, are not suitable for their oversized cars.

Now Laren is already busy as it is intersected by several roads, so there are a lot of buses, trucks and even tractors pass along the roads. Because of that, deep tracks are pulled through the streets.

That makes it dangerous for cyclists. They actually flirt with the death.

*

A lot of retirees in the Gooi discover a lot of great places to relax. Some even discover how great the ice creams and pancakes are in this place.

Retirees radiate satisfaction and they get to know quiet.

They also enjoy the surroundings and look surprised when they encounter a "known" Dutch as Hannah Montana or Gordon.

They also often visit historical places.

The famous folk dance group, **The Klepperman**, is established there. They hired a large group of actors that depict the unveiling of the village pump a hundred years ago. A huge crowd enjoyed this unique event, which was directed by Frits Spits, the famous radio reporter.

*

Because all those tourists and women are also a few **"Laarders"**, it is hard to determine the original population of the place.

The **"Larinesen"**, is the part of the population that lives in Laren, but did not originally come from there.

These are often well-off, but do not allow themselves to stand just anywhere. They seek proper contact and are often an incentive for all new developments.

Their children are at school in Laren and they own oversized cars, but in recent years, the modern tricycles became very "in". You will also see a lot of young mothers and au pairs with bicycles.

*

What all these people have in common is that they all need their daily shopping. You can always find them at the mall. It is truly a melting pot of all types (and more) than has already been described.

It's always very busy and everyone comes and goes.

But wherever you go, you will always pass by Ahmed, a homeless man. He has been there for so long.

Yes, you read that right; a homeless man in one of the richest towns in the Netherlands.

Everyone is very nice to him. They really treat him very kindly.

He is also very attentive and chats with everyone.

He is always remembered by everyone he had already seen. Especially women, young or old does not matter to him. They have a real soft spot for him.

He bows graciously and with keen interest to them. He greets them as if he confronts a years-lost relative.

They hold long conversations with him and pour their heart out many times; about the problems with their husband or boyfriend's infidelity; their children and grandchildren, how it went with tennis, and so on.

Ahmed actually has an antenna for such things. He does everything to create a good atmosphere: *"What a great granddaughter you have"* or *"How was it in the hospital?"* Or *"That's a cute dog, what's his name?"*

He just sits there waiting for people who knows him and would look him in the eye. After patiently waiting on his chair, he bounces up and launches a new slogan.

Soon, he became the popular homeless hugger.

*

After closing the mall they see him with tears in his eyes with his worn-out bike. Where would he go? Which bench would he sleep on? Under what overpass? Those were the questions that sat along the people's heads, but no answer really came.

THE END OF EVERYTHING

It had been a restless night in the Nursing House the Heul in Bussum. There was a great storm that raged, and no one was really able to sleep.

Everyone appeared to the inspection table looking pale and grumpy. They are all craving coffee and lots of coffee was really needed.

But it was very disappointing because there was no coffee. There was nothing for the lightning had struck, and all the equipment was burned. Even the toaster was broken.

Grandpa Kees turned on the television to see the news. There was no picture. Everything was black; same thing with the computer.

We all thought that the disaster was over, but the rain came back!

A violent storm broke loose again with intense lightning and heavy thunder.

The water streets went under the manhole covers and drifted around. Suddenly, water flowed along the walls. The roof was gone!

Everyone tried to save what they could, but the technical department came short of hands.

The wheelchairs plowed through the water and the boosters were like rowboats.

Fortunately, the occupants were unharmed, but the fear will be stuck in them.

Again, a lightning strike and the transformer of the house went on the air!

A moment later, a ball lightning trailed on the corridors of the building.

It seemed like there was a war going on in the Nursing House the Heul. It was very much different from the peaceful place that it used to be.

*

It was weeks later that everything was restored, as far as they could.

Luckily, there was coffee again.

At the end of the afternoon, while enjoying the Pickwick tea, the conversation turned to the state of the world and a book by Ludovic Kennedy.

Grandpa Kees had read about some kind of bomb that is being developed. It is a mixture of a chemical and a nuclear bomb. You just cannot imagine how dangerous it is.

It was really awful that terrorists wanted to change with war and attacking civilians. It was not a question of whether the bomb will be used. The question is, when?

Nurse Marijke thought that the conversation has become bleak, so she brought up a happier topic, but Grandpa Kees did not let the conversation end. He still talked about a weapon that is threatening to the humanity: **the electronic bomb.**

She just looked at him incredulously for bringing up things like that.

As if to put his words, there was a huge bright flash on the horizon, and all the lights went out.

As time went on, the first reports came in about the effects of these electronic bomb thrown by a few terrorists in **Media Park** in Hilversum.

Everything that needed electricity has stopped working; the power stations, telephone, and of course the Internet.

No one could access the Internet.

No one could be able to use their phones to call or text. In short, everyone and everything was unreachable. It was the 6 th of May, the day that the political Pim Fortuyn was murdered a few years ago.

According to rumors, it was because the former supporters of Pim started a revolution for his death anniversary. There was no improvement in the country, and because Pim is dead, no one would listen to them.

And now, **they have had enough.**

Meanwhile, the population was sitting with hands in their hair. They had all their files and photos on their remote computers stored safely somewhere in case their home computers crash, but now the world has become unreachable, and maybe even deleted!

The websites with their own profiles on YouTube, Hyves, and anywhere else, were inaccessible. They suddenly could no longer reach their virtual friends.

In short it was CHAOS, and it was getting worse as it took longer.

Everyone was forced to do everything manually again. They send letters physically; services were rendered with written banknotes, and so on.

The Army and Civil Defense had their hands full with the new situation. They still hunted for the revolutionaries, but they were all untraceable.

Everyone was just waiting for the next blow.

IT WAS THE END OF EVERYTHING.

*

Nurse Marijke shook with more strength and focused at what Grandpa Kees would say in his sleep.

He came to his senses and looked around, dazed.

"Where am I? What's happening?" he babbled in confusion and continued, *"What is Prime Minister Balkenende doing there on the TV? Was he not turn down? Are we still being attacked?"*

Slowly, very slowly, Grandpa Kees wakes up from a very bad dream.

SILENT WEEK

For centuries, people have many customary events when they stopped doing what they always do to celebrate solstice. Whether it was Christmas, Sylvester meetings, or any other traditional holidays, almost all religions celebrate.

There are events such as **the St. John's meeting** in Laren, and **St. John's procession** in the Gooi. It is the only procession of the Roman Catholic Church above the major rivers in the Netherlands. That is very special.

But this time, I want to reflect on the week that precedes it. The event is in-between the **Art Laren** and **Laren Fair**.

Art Laren is a three-day event on the Brink of Laren where all sorts of galleries from around the country show their collections. Thus, we read on the website of Art Laren:

"This year there were 24 galleries, and art from over 150 artists were showed. There were galleries from Spain and France. The pavilions of the artifacts were under the trees of the Brink. Despite the changeable weather, 12,000 visitors were counted.

The event was musically framed by students of the Utrecht Conservatory. The event ended by having the oldest band in the municipality of Laren play in the middle of the field.

The wine action for charity was a great success. More than 900 bottles were sold. Glossy interior design magazines were distributed.

Art Laren is an initiative of Kiwanis Club Laren, and is organized by a Foundation for Art Laren. The implementation is in the hands of the 25 members of the Kiwanis Club Laren. The net proceeds went to various charities."

Art Laren is a festive event, there are beautiful paintings and sculptures are showcased. Visitors come from all over.

The opening was over, and I strolled around from one gallery to the next. The exhibitors and their patrons drank a glass of white wine. The atmosphere was cozy.

Suddenly, a loud barking white Jack Russell terrier ran like crazy between the public from one end of the land to the other, tossing clouds of dust.

He kept running and he was not caught. He went out in the middle of the field and boldly looked at everyone. Everyone burst out laughing, and his owner hastened to put him on the leash and dragged him away.

But what was the root cause of all this? A few years before that, on the same spot where a Jack Russel race was held. Dozens of dogs ran like crazy.

They ran so fast that many dogs flew off the road, and it was an impressive sight.

The dog that flew about Art Laren probably had participated back then. His memory of it might have came up.

*

The week after Art Laren was the week for the St. John's procession and that was very different; no white wine, no flirting, no attention-grabbing celebs, and so on.

It was to devote and honor John the Baptist, who took care of the needy.

Laren was well aware of this.

The locals were busy with the preparations; the streets were decorated, the triumphal arches were placed, and the basilica was rigged.

The brides (young girls), who traditionally is part of the procession, were marching in their white dresses to practice.

Pastor Vriend was busy around the Good Shepherd Chapel.

The music association, MCC, exercised and checked all of the organists at the church.

Furthermore there was a worn atmosphere. They knew what was coming, and it is the Holy Week.

But as you may have noticed, Laren is also overwhelmed by the many visitors of the Singer Museum, and especially the many fashion shops. There are also the many Gooische Women who, like the visitors, populate the streets and terraces.

They are more than welcome, because they give the local economy a boost. It is so severe that without them, the stores would not have existed.

But in this Holy Week, everything is a bit stark.

While the carillon sounds are scattered about Laren, a white carriage drawn by six horses moved through the streets with a swinging couple on board. Six footmen dressed in bright red uniforms supervise the whole procession.

On the way to the Basilica, came along the closed **Grand Café Aubère**. The landlord had been following the operator out. He had no confidence in him because of the many debts that he had.

Aside from the debts, he was also not able to pay tax.

It was tough, what happened. The contract documents were snatched from his hands and the tables were taken away from them. There they were beaten and dumbfounded, while the mayor and other bystanders watched, stunned.

After a few weeks, there had been a reopening of the Grand Cafe, but unfortunately that did not last long.

The terrace of Mauve ogled. I ordered a cappuccino and looked at the public. Women looked longingly at the men, trying to pull through by talking. Some are constantly in their mobile phones.

I could go on and on about what I see, but what it comes down to is that all of these things are in stark contrast with the Holy Week and with the Procession of St. John's on Sunday.

After that week, is the Laren Fair. It is full of party and entertainment. It's held on the first Monday of July. It has been a tradition for decades and it's always great to take part in it.

This year, the event was given an extra dimension with a special mass. It was headed by Chaplain Van Welzenes and concelebrant, Pastor Vriend. The music was taken care of by Laren's St. John's Conservatory.

It was very special to start the event that way.

POWER OF SMALL THINGS

It was still early, so I took a bike ride along the edges of the Gooi. The sun was just rising above the horizon and lit up the sheep on the dike. In the distance, a lonely farmer was plowing his field.

The tour began in Naarden through the Old Valkeveen.

I enjoyed cycling around the Gooi because of its wonderful nature.

There was a morning mist which the sun poked around. A few fishermen had already taken their place on the shore.

In the distance, the mills were running a bit tired, but were still put in motion by the morning breeze.

It had apparently rained, so I saw a rainbow against a dark sky.

I continued cycling until I reached Lage Vuursche, where I took the time to enjoy a cup of coffee.

After that, I went near the airport in Hilversum. There were a lot of planes and they were all such a sight to see.

I went further to Loosdrecht, along that is a long dike to the Driesprong. I went right into Ankeveen, the place with the best skating rink in the Gooi lies.

I went by the Graveland, Spanderswoud, and then had another cup of coffee in a little pub at the Crailose Bridge, and then St. Janskerkhof (the cemetery of St. John's Church), where a geological museum was established. The place would hold a lecture about the origin of Hilversum.

We were put in a circle and a guide began talking about the history with a legend called:

Hille for the Sum

Many believe that the name Hilversum came from the legend, "Hille for the sum." In the village of Laren, there was a girl named Hille. Her father was heavily addicted to gambling and was often completely broke. One night, he went out to gamble in exchange for his daughter. When Hille found out about is, she immediately decided to leave Laren with anger and sadness. She met a young farmer named Hilfert. Together, they went towards the hill and found a farm somewhere in a valley. At that time, the farm was called farmyard, but it eventually became Hilferts Hilversum.

According to another version of the legend, Hille met the two gods, Wodan and Braga. Hille complained to them about how her father treats her. Both were furious and Wodan had said with his trembling voice, "Curse you, Laer. Curse you, who squanders and sell his own child. Never will you have great wealth. You will always fail! My blessing will rest on another village to be built. It shall be called Hille-for-the-sum. It is where your daughter live, and that village will be the largest and richest in Nardinckland.

After the curse, Braga speaks, "Poor Laer… Poor Laer I can be the bane of the mighty Wodan, my father, do not turn away. But Braga gives you, the god of the singers and the magical storytellers: once great artists will live in your little houses…So mote it be!"

And so Hilversum was established and had grown. Laren remained small, but with many artists, singers and yuppies!

It's funny, but it's OK.

*

During my bike ride, which led me further to Table Mountain, it dawned on me how beautiful everything looked in the Gooi.

Its nature has been shaped by years of purchase of natural areas. A significant portion of the surface, which is about 60% of the current approximately 2,700 acres, came in the hands of the Gooische Nature Reserve in 1933. This organization was founded a year earlier to maintain the natural beauty of the Gooi.

This foundation has also started small, and that is something that strikes me again and again. The most important things start small.

It was time for lunch and I settled down to the pool of a half-empty cup of coffee on the terrace of the restaurant at the Tafelberg (Table Mountain).

After that, I enjoyed a delicious omelet, which I washed down with a glass of milk.

Satisfied, I looked around and saw workmen.

At first I did not understand it, but the waitress was kind enough to explain it.

It turned out that a few months ago the Sheepfold, with over a hundred of sheep, was previously burned. It was on a middle of the night and it happened so fast that everything was irretrievably lost.

Those who were there still shuddered at the memory of the screams of those poor beasts.

It was all because of an arsonist who had never been arrested.

The place was quite a loss for everybody.

There are many well-off in that area, but there was one that cut the knot, so one hundred thousand Euros became available to finance a new sheepfold.

Soon, everything is ready, and then everyone can again enjoy the place.

*

Of course I had to go to Table Mountain. It was much lower than I expected. It was the highest point of the Gooi-country (36.4 m above sea level), but still.

The last time I was there, I was a Boy Scout.

The view was beautiful; flowering heaths, endless trails, beautiful forests, and rolling countryside. You could also see well all the towns and villages.

I quickly whizzed down the slope on the way to Blaricum and thought how often a single person could make a difference; Zweitzer Albert, Mandela, Obama and so on.

They had/have so many forces in motion that it seemed like they have super strengths, but that was not so. They were/are inspiring personalities that give us hope and initiate movements.

Blaricum is small but cozy. I stopped at the Woensberg and took a walk to enjoy the nature, and then I went ahead and stopped at the terrace restaurant, Rust Wat.

It's a place you will never forget! An old rustic restaurant with a beautiful terrace is there, next to the skating rink of Blaricum. If there is no frost, it is a beautiful lake with a small island where occasional outdoor concerts are held.

Nature is wonderfully there and one can enjoy some of the finest and tastiest food and drink.

Last winter weather, it was possible to skate there. It was a feast for the eyes!

*

On the way home, I passed the Brink of Laren, where there is a large skating rink. They called it "Skating on the Brink".

It was in the initiative of three ladies who wanted to get back the old image of skating in Brink.

The opening was done by some famous Larinesen, DJ Erik de Zwart, and singer, Jeroen van der Boom. The latter even gave a spontaneous performance. It was so great!

Tens of thousands had come down on the skating rink, its success was unbelievable. All schools go there with their students for skating. Some even celebrate their birthdays there.

It proves that the power of the small things make a difference and always will!

SAINT JOHN'S PROCESSION

St John's Procession is one of the most important religious processions in our country. It is the only religious ceremony outside the public road, going up the great rivers of the Netherlands.

This is in memory of a robbery where three sullen women had their breasts cut off. Laar founded the chapel in the village. Three times at night, the bell would be ringed. It was a divine sign that there is a chapel in the area. Outside the village is St John's Cemetery. It has been around since the 1600s.

In the 18th century, the Brotherhood of Saint John was born. In the 19th century the pilgrimage became a joint tour, where crosses and banners were carried. From the second half of the 19th century, Laren managed the route they travel. Initially, they carried banners made from colored wools, and crosses made of branches or wood. Now, they carry yellow-white flags, wooden and metal pomp arches, and flowers.

As of 1886, the pilgrimage became a sacrament of procession. The chapel at St. John's cemetery dates from the late 19th century, and in 1924, the St. John church was built.

The procession takes place annually on the Sunday that is closest to the 24th of June. On Friday, the arches builders begin. On Saturday, there is a trip by carriage along the arcs. On Sunday, a mass starts at 9:00 am. The procession pulls out at 11.00 and ends around 14.00 back into the church. It is when the Saint John's Song was sung.

*

The famous book, "The Testimony on the Street", gives us a glimpse of that wonderful event in Laren.

If you do not like the Catholic procession, once you see and experience it, you will just really admire how everyone makes everything happen. You will also admire the amount of visitors that came to witness the procession and for their own faith.

The thing that surprised me is the simplicity and the simple notion of God which bind them.

In addition, led by the full Board of Mayor and Aldermen, they all went with their partners.

Furthermore, there are many dignitaries including representatives of the Royal Family and the army.

The event is accompanied by great music. The procession is also accompanied by leaders of Catholic guilds and associations, with their huge banners. In the middle of the procession is the

Bishop of Haarlem under a canopy with the sign of St. John on his hand.

One goes to St. John, takes the communion, and then comes back to the Basilica. The gathered crowd flows under the Basilica; chiming in and is being addressed by the Bishop of Haarlem.

The church was packed with everyone from all ages, countries, sizes, and so on.

At such a moment, you would think of the Biblical words:

"Blessed are the simple-minded."

*

The sunlight shone through the stained glass windows. The people felt that they were touched by their creator. **His light shone on them.**

A miracle occurred; the transformation. The mighty organ played **Te Deum** with innumerable voices.

The choirs take the lead, the organ is assisted by a band, and the walls of the Basilica vibrate.

Then the touching song, **Tantum Ergo,** played. After a final salute and thanks from the Bishop, attacks the trumpets of the band and the church organ would play once again with the intro to the final song, the famous **Laren Saint John Song.**

The music that blared through the space seemed to be directly addressed to Heaven, in knowing that He listens and is with them.

Thousands of voices sang that beautiful song and it echoed through the vaults, with the sound of a mighty organ.

And then it's over: the people goes back to where they came from, strengthened and united. Until next year!

ARABIC INFLUENCES

It's been almost three years ago when a journalist uttered all sorts of curses and had thrown a pair of shoes on President George Bush during a press conference in Iraq.

Bush was able to dodge the shoes, but the picture was put down. A lot of people in Iraq hated the U.S.

It became quite a hype on the internet. There were even mini games wherein you could throw virtual shoes on Bush.

This afternoon, a strange thing happened to me. When I casually strolled through the streets, I saw a woman with great speed run out of a house, with a shoe in one hand. On the other hand was a bag full of shoes.

She ran around the Torenlaan, and then began to throw shoes on the traffic while shouting profanities.

I rubbed my eyes, this could not be true. The event three years ago could have had this effect and that was almost unthinkable, but it was happening.

After her rage, she returned to her house with an empty bag. I could not help but ask her motives.

"Of course, it's that damn traffic," she impatiently replied. She explained that she was not able to sleep last and other nights because of the continuous traffic.

I left her, but only because there was nothing to really talk about. She went back inside trying to find more shoes.

But it was a clear sign; something must be done to increase traffic, otherwise serious accidents will happen!

BURNING MESSAGES

Fire Department in the Gooi sends Fire Trucks Away.

Published 08 Nov 2011 Gooi and Eemlander | 16:05

A total of nine fire engines will be sold by March next year because of budget cutbacks in Gooi and Vecht.

The cuts are a result of the financial crisis. The fire departments in Gooi and Vecht did not expect any problems would be caused if they got rid of those fire engines despite the series of arson in Huizen and Laren.

Half -Thatched Roof Lost in Big Fire in Blaricum.

Published on November 13, 11Gooi Eemlander, 08:48.

Last updated November 13, 11, 11:32

BLARICUM - The fire department was alerted shortly before eight o'clock on a Sunday morning for a big fire at a mansion in the Melkweg in Blaricum. Two hours later, the roof still smoldered. The fire department was able to save the house by making a hole center through the roof. A

handful of firemen helped, and as a result, half of the roof was lost.

Along the Melkweg, a leafy avenue in Blaricum, are numerous thatched buildings. One of the houses has caught on fire. Same house also caught on fire last February 27.

Assistance from neighboring police forces, like ones in Laren and Hilversum Nederhorst den Berg came.

Six arrested after traffic hassle.

Published by Editor De Gooi-en Eemlander Published November 13, 11, 21:42

Last updated November 13, 11, 22:29

BLARICUM - Six people were arrested on a Sunday afternoon in Blaricum. It was due to a collision that occurred in Torenlaan.

Presumably, the drivers were fighting while on the road. It deliberately caused a collision, as reported by the spokeswoman of the police. After the collision, the fight continued on the street. It included a total of five people. The sixth was someone who just got involved.

Huge Fire on a Timber Trade in Laren.

Published on November 13, 11 Gooi Eemlander, 23:14

Last updated November 14, 11, 06:28

BROKERS - Update Video - Van Dijk's Timber Trade caught on fire Last Sunday at quarter to eleven in the evening. A timber that was located on the middle of the area, caught on fire and began the huge fire.

The fire can be seen at the sky even miles away from Laren. The fire department has deployed large equipment's to fight the fire from a fuel tank that has exploded.

Residents of the neighboring houses were forced to leave their homes and evacuated in the former town hall. Around one o'clock, the danger was over. One person became ill and was taken to the hospital by ambulance.

The entrepreneur Mathijs de Roos lost his surveillance connection from his home. Moments later, he was notified of the fire that was going on. He rushed from to the Gooi and saw, to his horror that the building where his construction company stood was on fire.

"I've probably lost everything. Maybe there are some documents left, but I doubt it. Because of this fire, there is not much left."

The site, since March of this year, has been owned by MBB Development of Maarssen. Twenty apartments are to be built in the area. The St. John library is also to be demolished to be a part of the project.

A Fire Wall of a Hundred Meters

Published by Editor De Gooi-en Eemlander, Published November 14, 11, 11:53

Last updated November 14, 11, 13:11

LAREN - A fire wall of a hundred meters in the area of Van Dijk' sawing mill occurred last Sunday night.

Several managers of Laren let themselves in similar terms if they look back at the turbulent night. They were just going to bed or were on the verge of doing so, like Angelique van de Kerkhof. She was still sitting behind her laptop around eleven when all of a sudden; there was an orange glow across the street that was quickly expanding. She brought her photo albums into safety. Her roommate kept the thatch wet. The chickens flew into the tree. "I barely knew that they could fly," she says.

The Laren fire department soon realized that the wind was making the fire worse. A neighbor came up with a bottle of vodka to keep her warm. Rika Peter (83), was found on the ground in the shaft. She once lived right next to the stables. In the early seventies, they had to leave because Mr. Van Dijk of timber rental withdrew.

LAREN- RTV NH

Residents of Laren were forced to leave their houses in the middle of the night last Sunday because of a nearby fire in the lumber yard. They were able to return to their homes on Monday.

84

"The area around the company is safe again," said a spokeswoman for the municipality.

The fire at the Zijtak began Sunday night, around eleven thirty, and was so severe that several corps of Utrecht had come to help. Units from Baarn, Soest, Woudenberg, and Amersfoort were also sent off to the Gooi.

Dozens of houses with thatched roofs were evacuated because they were threatened by blowing fire particles. Sixteen people were in the town and later stayed in a hotel. One person was startled by the fire and had chest pain. The current in parts of Laren fell briefly.

MAYOR`s WORK

In the whole range of professions that exist, there are many that speak to the imagination, especially being a mayor.

It gives a person that feeling of being a father to many citizens; a family man who has an eye for everyone; a real father figure.

Whether a person has that quality, the real question is, whether he or she qualifies to be a striking mayor.

In this time, it is impossible to carry out this function. The standards and requirements got higher. Apart from those things, candidates are also weighed by the political parties that they are representing.

A real mayor is supposed to stand above the parties; to connect and reconcile everyone.

Mayors in the Gooi came from different political parties.

There is a democratic organization that has been around for centuries. They are known as the **Erfgooiers.**

Erfgooiers has been around since the middle ages in the lands owned by Abbey of Elten (now located in Germany). During the reign of the Count of Holland, around 1300, the Gooi Marke came about. This was an agricultural interest group, with the main objective to preserve, in perpetuity, the common land of the Gooi. The brand also got a name: Town and Country Gooiland. They had to also make sure that not too many newcomers will get the rights to the land. Eventually, two types of Erfgooiers emerged: the switch running and non-running switch.

This organization was a kind of inter-municipal organization.

This cooperation always remained very large and many things were agreed well by one another.

The mayor of Laren is a true liberal in the middle and has studied history, his name is Elbert Roest.

He's a nice, charming and erudite man who has a unifying effect on the population.

Not only by virtue of his position, but also because he enjoys what he does intensely. He's almost always present at the major and minor events in his village.

We saw him coming along in the previous chapter, but he was also at the opening of the **Laren Fair.** He stood there in shorts and baked donuts for the public together with the singer Willeke Alberti.

As you already know, art plays an important role in Laren. There are various activities throughout the year such as the Atelier Route, Art Laren, and everything that happens in Singer.

The name **Atelier Route** says it all. It is a route through the village to the various artists' studios and exhibition spaces.

A lot of people would go there because it is a unique opportunity to see the painters and sculptors in their own environment.

It is often breathtakingly beautiful.

Art Laren is different. It is an immense indoor exhibition in Brink.

Artists from all over the country have fought for months to get a spot on that event.

Hospitality is also present. They have hired the famous pub and they have great music to match everything.

Every money spent for it was worth it because it's all so beautiful.

Our mayor is always there to show his genuine interest.

The annual **Uitmarkt** gives an idea of what to do next season in the theaters. **Theatre Singer** has a reputation to maintain, and there is always something new in that place.

The season begins traditionally with **Laren Jazz.** Known musicians play on that event.

The entire building and garden are in use, and the hospitality is abundant. It is a very busy event. People come from across the country for their favorite musician or band.

And guess who saunters there with a beer in his hand? You guessed it right.

In Laren, we also know about the **Gooi Academy.** It is where one can get painting and sculpture classes. Mainly ladies are the ones enrolled in the lessons. They are all easy to recognize in Mauve. They usually have large folders with them, containing their newest artwork.

*

Of course, the political control of the municipality is also part of the job of the mayor. He works in the council and outside with the political parties.

The largest group is **Larens Conservation.** The local party is led by Councilor Leo Jansen.

Laren works closely with neighboring municipalities like Blaricum and Eemnes. They formed a cheaper and more efficient management. They are called the **BEL municipality.** There is a communal hall built for them, but in their own places, a municipal office remains available.

The combined population of the government employees in the three towns was still small; about 30,000 people.

Laren has a **political café,** which is held monthly at the famous Café het Bonte Paard (The Spotted Horse).

One time Wouter Bos of the Labour Party came to explain the credit crisis of many investors in the church. Mark Rutten of the Liberal Party would also come to discuss the critical cracks on integration. A lot of speakers would attend that meeting. The mayor is always present at that.

In Theater Singer, consultation evenings were held for a new **structural concept** development for Laren. Aldermen and the board of the mayor would always be present in those evenings. That was sometimes hard, because once they speak their unwillingness or problems about the proposed terms, no one would actually go against them.

It was fascinating evenings, but the result of all this participation remains to be unseen.

*

There are also events of a more personal nature in which the mayor is involved, such as anniversaries and awarding ceremonies.

You would see him take pictures with a lot of villagers. It was often in the local village newspaper.

But this mayor of Laren never stops.

Laren was ravaged by an arsonist who often targets thatched houses.

The mayor is always in those areas to reassure everyone that they are doing the best they could to get a hold of the suspect and to keep everyone safe.

Even with the return of local sports heroes, he never let himself not witness the whole thing.

Together with them, they would ride around a village; doing a motorcade to be welcomed by the people.

*

Every time an activity is opened, it is attended by the mayor. He always aims to unite what was divided. He has a great job and he enjoys it. He is right for the job.

CROSSROAD OF THE MOST EXPENSIVE

"Once the reason that Laren's hockey moms still just in Volvo station wagons, is because the wealthy dads moved around in BMWs, Jaguars or - if they were a dentist or surgeon - a Saab (Turbo).

Okay, Laren knew one exception: the gentleman with the white Rolls Royce and gold watch. He turned out to be a former brothel owner, and was later condemned as a launderer of the biggest drug lords in the Netherlands. In its wake, from the late eighties, the tires were getting wider and the exhaust louder.

Meanwhile the driving equipment is so exclusive that every weekend, a group of at least ten car spotters run around the area. "A Range Rover or a Volkswagen; you can see hundreds of those on an afternoon, so I never need to look for one," says Kevin Large, who is regularly in Laren. "You would come against real exotics like Bugatti Veyron (1 million +) or the Porsche Carrera GT. There is no other place in Netherlands that you would always see those."

Inspired by his enthusiasm, I started to tally. I strategically sat between men and ladies at the Café het Bonte Paard. From the terrace, I counted 67 (different!) Range Rovers, 34 Porsches, 23 BMW (7 series), 13 Mercedes S-class, 37 Jaguars, 4 Ferraris, 5 Aston Martins, 6 Bentley's 3 Maserati's, and a Corvette. And oh yeah, a Rene Froger, who was driving his aging red Bentley.

According to my calculator, I had seen more than 27 million in luxury cars in just 2.5 hours.

Published by Dagblad De Pers, July 19, 2011; by Edward Deiters

*

This notice in the newspaper immediately attracted my attention when I opened the paper. I immediately got all kinds of thoughts and visions.

So there were 194 expensive cars averaging roughly 140,000 euros that are sold within a minute. The cheaper models were left out, so can you imagine what drove around there.

But if we focus on the pricier models, I thought about how many cheaper cars you could buy with that amount of money. That would be 3370 Peugeot 107, a model that is currently economically best-selling.

1 out of 3 people of Laren (11,500 inhabits) would buy such cars; both children and elderly included.

You could give all the 5,500 households electric Golf carts with that money.

Also, in there, you could buy good bikes for the whole population of Bussum (27,000).

Many of those cars are hobby cars or second cars, so you can see what a huge fleet in Laren is present.

But if you really think about it, we could help the people in Africa with 18 million Euros, while driving in Laren for about 2 hours on the Brink! Shocking.

A SATISFIED SMOKER

On this day of November last year, we said goodbye to autumn. The sun was shining and it was such a pleasure. Nothing pointed to the approaching winter cold.

I came up with the concept of **"a satisfied smoker is not a troublemaker".**

In addition to the roundabout on the Torenlaan in Laren, is a group of impressive century-old trees. They are standing majestically against the sky and show us how beautiful nature is.

There were two trees with roots close to each other. There was a young blond woman with her back against one tree and her legs leaning against another tree, as if it were a hammock.

She lay there under the sunlight. Her whole demeanor spoke of a perfect contentment.

Apparently nothing seems to bother her. Not the onslaught of the traffic or even a street dog that sniffed her. She was alone in her own world.

Suddenly, she took a cigarette from her mouth and blew a nice cloud of smoke. She looked happy after the puff and smiled at nature, to herself, and to her happiness.

She remained the way she was until she finished her cigarette. She slowly stood up and walked in the direction of Blaricum. It's a pity that Minister Schippers of Health Care did not see this.

THE GOOI DECENCY

A tile with inscription for Elena

Published on November 8, 11 and Gooi-en Eemlander, 16:48

Last updated on November 8th 11, 19:06 Gooi-en Eemlander

"What we have done is unique," says spokesman Alexander Bunt in behalf of Dudok Wonen. "It's a matter of piety."

A topic of discussion is the grave of Elena Arkadjevna Gengrinovich, a Russian who was came to Hilversum. She lived in an apartment of the Dudok Wonen Corporation on Eagle Street.

The woman made a name in her native country before leaving for the Netherlands as a concert pianist. She chose to end her life at home. She was divorced and had a daughter in Israel, whom she had no contact with.

Elena Gengrinovich had laid for more than a month in her apartment. On October 3, she was found dead. She remained nameless for several weeks for no one came forward to claim her body. The municipality was held responsible for her burial, but it was said that they had no money for an inscribed stone.

In the article in this newspaper were comments from people who felt that the woman had earned more than an unmarked grave. That was also said by the fortune teller, with whom Elena called regularly for the last two years before her death and then extensively talked about her life. This woman, who calls himself Apollonia, put her tarot cards and tried to prevent Elena from taking away her own life.

Dudok Wonen came into the scene and had an internal discussion to "dress up" the grave. The corporation funded the whole thing.

THE FESTIVAL WILL BEGIN

It's that time again!

The most important period of the year has arrived: the party in December.

Last Saturday we were all welcome Santa-Claus, this Saturday was a festive manner super cozy rink opened on the Brink.

Under the motto "SKATING ON THE BRINK" had some ladies three years ago, took the initiative to restore. An old tradition uncountable had already found this unique place in the Gooische Laren their little ones to deliver. Unforgettable hours

Three years ago, the opening was graced by Jeroen van der Boom, and now Gordon and LA The Voices did a spectacular performance. Gordon commemorated the deceased rather enjoyed this week Coco Meyere appropriately: What a tragic end of a seemingly beautiful life that they themselves put an end badly!

The whole village Laren has been transformed into a real winter landscape: countless lights are on in the many trees and facades. The shops invite you to make purchases and look great.

Many shuffling along the facades and many credit cards is red hot.

Tomorrow, Sunday, is a shopping Sunday and it will be much busier and thus gradually to the St. Nicholas and Christmas then it will get worse.

Buses bring groups of tourists, so you can hear the one time and then the Twents, Fries or Limburg dialect.

It is a festive season which will start and Laren is again an oasis in a country that is in crisis.

MATTER OF CHOOSING

Nov. 5 - The coalition parties in Laren support the massive tax increase that the council will impose on the property tax (14.6%) on 2012. Were their backs against the wall because of the closure of the asylum center? Not really. During the fiscal council yesterday, they revealed that the college's property tax increased based on a doomsday scenario. If all applicants were away on January 1, 2012 (tally date population Laren rich pay benefits) than sitting alderman Evert de Jong with a gap of four tons. Only that's not likely. The closure is only in the course of next year. Laren and calls itself at the organization of refugees to a humane reduction. Considering young people who still have to do exams and elderly people for whom good health should be guaranteed. "Crailo going than planned, a few months earlier near a token woman on the property tax increase," noted Jacqueline Timmerman (opposition Liberal Laren). "Because if it is that bad then the property tax is not reduced. Why not first six percent?" May parliamentary leader of the liberal VVD party Mr. Polano (Coalition Party) was honest about. "Because of the euro crisis, there is a willingness to accept for load increased. Therefore, we must now address the increase." Moreover, the euro in the near future is vital. Especially between 2014 and 2016 when the church is not accorded more jobs through decentralization but not **correspondingly filled bags with money.**

Peter Calis (Larens Preservation Coalition Party) downplayed the draconian measures in austere times. "For a house of a million is about 2.40 euros a week."

D66 had CBS figures. But to refute that Laren its property tax rate is lagging behind compared to other municipalities. According to these figures, Laren already, without the 14.6% (13% for the hole of four tons plus inflation), a property tax-topper in the Gooi region. With 622 per household.

Second after notorious leader Blaricum (926 euros) and above Naarden (539), Muiden (520), Eemnes (437) and Hilversum (393). "And the sewage goes up by 36%," added Nico Wegter (D66) to. There was a tsunami of motions and amendments. The VVD was Larens Conservation of support for additional cuts in 2013 (150.000 euros) in 2014 (250.000) and 2015 (350,000). Where the knife concretely should go, it is decided at the request of Conservation Larens later.

Source: Gooi en Eemlander.

*

Question:

Where is the increase in the budget that was created by the advent of the Asylum Centre at that time? Is it not reversed?

This goes against every budget line.

This temporary windfall should be kept separated and should not have been outside the regular budget of the municipality.

SENIOR SOCIETY

New! Seniors' Private Day Care Center in Laren.

Dear reader(s),

The population of the retirees is growing and there is a huge shortage of day care for seniors.

As of September 1, 2011, the picturesque village of Laren (NH), will open a day care for the seniors.

As of that date, Seniors Society of Laren opens its doors in a historic and unique thatched farmhouse located in the city center.

We cater to seniors who have a need for companionship, with mild somatic limitations, and the chronically ill or with starting psychogeriatric problems. We assist seniors who want to give structure to their daily lives. Also, our guests can continue to live with us.

We are open from 10:00 in the morning until 16:00 in the afternoon. In terms of structure, Senior Society-Laren is similar to a nursing home. The big difference is the luxury, location, care, the presence of a small permanent team, and that our guests have a safe and pleasant environment. We also provide the (hot) lunch. Our regular hostesses offer our guests a variety of activities it goes without saying that we also take care of transportation to and from the home address.

We give our daycare realized in two phases. Phase 1 is during the workweek. We get 8 to 10 guests in a homely and welcoming atmosphere. In phase 2, we will once again provide an additional 12 to 15 more guests.

Want to know more? Look at www.seniorensocieteit-laren.nl or call tel 06 44,211,458.

You can also send an email to info@seniorensocieteit-laren.nl.

*

The above newspaper article in the Gooi-en Eemlander of July 13, 2011 struck me in a special way.

It demonstrates the changes at this time. The aging population seems to have new needs. The article reveals a serious approach and we wish them every success with their business.

But it also puts us thinking that in Laren, more than 50% of the population aged 65 and above. It is the city with most aging people in our country.

In Laren, there are numerous residential and nursing homes of high quality. The Rosa Spier House is well known, as well as Theodotion and Stichtse Hof. Those three are within 1000 feet close together.

On the Eemnesserweg is Johanneshove and just outside the city limits is the Torenhof.

These are all nursing homes.

There was still Trappenberg Rehabilitation, Hospital Tergooi, the Blind Institute Visio, Asthma Centre Heideheuvel and a few more.

Then there are the home care agencies as well.

Overall, the needs of the retired people can be properly taken care of.

And now a private initiative: the Senior Society Laren. It sounds like a good initiative, but it makes us realize how our society is rapidly changing. If you walk around Laren, you would have to be very cautious, because there are a lot of old people driving around the area.

It's all good and it's nice that the older people could survive in our hometown as well as elsewhere, but the development just makes you think.

So very soon, sidewalks suitable for walkers and wheelchairs would moat probably be made.

And then there is the ice control. It is shameful that in one of the wealthiest communities in our country, sidewalks and roads are impassable in winter conditions.

Finally, there will be many hands that will be needed to meet the increasing demand for care. It is a real growth market with room for new creative ideas and Seniors Society is one of them. We wish them luck!

KNOWLEDGE INCREASE SORROW

The **"Society Jan Hamdorff"** of Laren has the motto: "Go on to Laren".

This gentlemen's club is derived from the well-known pub in Hamdorff. The hangout "The pub" has always been the center of social life.

What's special was that, the pub is something of pure bohemian. Among other things, reflected amicable intercourse between people of all walks of life.

That was a common feature of life in Laren.

The environment still has something peculiar, something unique, and something special that was or is not found elsewhere. Everyone survives and lives with each other; they are all comfortable with each other.

The pure mutual cordiality has become a lot less, but the continuation of the pub in the Society Jan Hamdorff is still alive. Since its inception in 1959, the Society succeeded in that special atmosphere and culture of the pub.

Men from all walks of life meet there in that special and unique institution.

*

Today there was a guest speaker from a fellow club in Hilversum. It has been long awaited because he would speak on the theme "Knowledge Makes More Smart." A somewhat mysterious theme, one could not imagine what good it would pass.

It was not often that a speaker normally kept people engaged in bridge, billiards and hang out at the bar.

But the president had insisted that there is also an occasional speaker who would come to give a new impetus.

At 8:30, it was time. The guest speaker was inside and entered the pulpit.

He was a neatly dressed and coiffed man, but clearly of a different national character.

He spoke flawless Dutch and introduced himself as Mr. Mehmet. Then he began his argument.

He introduced himself by telling his life story. For five years, he lived in the Netherlands and came from Iran.

He had attended high school and attended the University, where he graduated as a psychologist in there.

For years, he had a psychotherapy practice, but he became more fascinated by politics.

Iran began, at that time, their revolution to escape from the Shah of Persia. After only a few years in the parliament, the country had gradually become more and more restless. There was a bloody and brutal war with neighboring Iraq, and many of his friends were killed. And there was an ongoing power struggle between the clergy and politicians.

But he came to the surface and even became mayor of a medium-sized city.

In his spare time, he was Imam, because Islam had always fascinated him.

Suddenly, fate had struck. His wife has committed adultery and was arrested.

He knew what awaited her. She would be buried up to her chest and stoned until she was dead.

There was no escape, the Sharia's was clear on this, and whether he was a mayor and an Imam, it made no difference.

*

Something snapped in him. He loved his wife and was willing to forgive her, but that did not matter. Her fate was certain.

It would happen in the town square of the city of which he was mayor.

And so it happened

He became all alone. He always helped people to accept their difficulties in life and to strike a new path. He always preached peace and rejected hatred. His wife is death by the sharia.

He was a man who many people had to support. His hair was snow white in one night and he spoke no more.

*

He no longer felt at home in Iran. His country had betrayed him, so he decided to leave. He did not care where, but he wanted a new start.

And so he ended up in Hilversum and became continue being an Imam.

He slowly recovered. He was a frequent speaker to make connections between the traditional and progressive Islam.

He was not looking for confrontation, but acceptance.

With these words he closed his introduction and the audience remained silent, impressed by what they had heard.

The mayor of Laren was also present. He was naturally curious about the experiences of his former colleague from Iran.

There were actually remarkable similarities that this country had with Iran. It's just that there is no summary execution in Laren.

*

Suddenly there was a comment from the back room with the question of whether he was sometimes known by Ahmed, who was homeless at the mall.

"Yes," was the unexpected answer *"In fact, I am Ahmed".*

Everyone was shocked with what he said.

It was a big controversy, but it turned out to be true.

The psychologist, who had become a mayor and Imam in his homeland, lived here to be a homeless at the Mall of Laren.

It was his way to leave the past behind and start over. He even hoped to take his old profession, but right now, he is still satisfied with this.

Now they also understood where his great strength to communicate came from. It was why we so wanted to talk to him. He is a psychologist.

The evening ended with a call from Ahmed to love our neighbor.

His final words were: *"Look at what unites people and take away what divides them."*

He left all attendees dumb and beaten back.

Hotel Hamdorff, Laren, Gooi

THE STICHTSE HOF

In the previous chapters, you almost forget that there is also another side to life; that of the neighbor who is facing his weaknesses as illness or discomfort.

Sooner or later we come in contact with it, and it's not always a pleasant acquaintance. They often experience loneliness and a sense of powerlessness. They became dependent on the assistance, whether it is provided in a nursing home or a hospital.

Many healthcare institutions offer whatever level the necessary assistance is.

This means there is a huge job, which years ago, I was allowed to take part of.

After having worked in accountancy, I became a junior clerk for 21 years in the Geriatric Nursing House the Stichtse Hof in Laren. It was during that time that the wages were paid in cash in those clear plastic bags every week.

It was the start of geriatrics health care and the buildings were not as bad as it is now.

The AWBZ (National insurance contributions) had just been established. (Ca 1965)

A geriatric patient is very restless and constantly looking for the exit, but it cannot if the door is locked. The rattling of the doors was, therefore, all day.

But for a young man of my age back then, I did great. I was with my family and friends. I was a junior clerk, but as my studies progressed, I was promoted to the position of administrator.

To persuade them to pay wages was always exciting.

The Stichtse Hof was expanded from 125 to 250 places and gave back a completely different dimension.

But what left an indelible impression were the events with residents / patients / clients.

The original nursing home was so large. There were 100 places allocated to residents of the city of Utrecht. There was one serious shortage of geriatric places. However, some came from the William Arntz Foundation, but they were not really geriatric patients, but elderly psychiatric patients.

Geriatric residents could only go outside under supervision, but the old inhabitants of the William Arntz Foundation were usually able to be with the society to move.

There was the duo Van der Sluis and Overdijkink, the first in a wheelchair. They constantly roamed the area and the village. They became a household name. On many terraces, they were to be found. Mr. Van der Sluis had the habit of sitting down at the street to view everything in his wheelchair.

At one point there was an indignant lady on the door that brought a jacket for him. She said it was a disgrace to just leave him out in the cold. We tell him it was better no longer to stay at the street.

Another resident and linen lady fell in love and they started a relationship.

Every day a demented notary came to our office that he was allowed to work there.

We placed him at an empty desk, gave him paper, pen, and a cup of coffee. He just wrote things on paper and mumbled things to himself. When the "work" was finished, he came back the next day.

There is much to tell about that period, but I want to take out the two most salient events.

*

One day, my eye struck by the lady who Mr. Meijer pulled painstakingly out of a car. Miss De Klerk was his housekeeper. Now, she was totally immobile.

What were they doing anyway? The next day, the garden boss, Mr. Grondman, asked me if I knew. The two got married

117

and their names were on the notice board of the Municipality of Laren.

Urgent consultation with the Director of Physician Sauer was the result, because this was obviously crazy. It was called by the Population Division, and after some time, came the message that the marriage would not get in the way of anything that is legal.

A few weeks later, a car service stopped at the door. It was the son of Mr. Meijer, a professional police commissioner in Nijmegen. I immediately began to pour his coffee and after some time, I asked if he had heard the big news.

It turned out he did not know. Furious, he stormed out the door to be on his way to the town hall. Never have we heard anything more.

Not long after, Mr. Meijer died, but Miss De Klerk could then continue to live in their house. That was the goal, and that was achieved. At that time this was the only solution for these situations.

Years later, I saw her in Utrecht, still dressed in her duffel coat.

*

The other event was Mr. Jacob. He also came from the Willem Arntz Foundation. He had lived there since the First

World War. Mr. Jacob was wounded in the war and as a result, he became disabled and no one has heard talk him since that day.

He helped Mr. Grondman to rake in the greenhouse every day. He was the only one who had some kind of contact with him.

Whether it was hot or cold, it did not matter if you looked out the window and see Mr. Jacob with his rake, a silent long tawny man wrapped in a thin grubby raincoat. Tragic.

Before the entry into force of the AWBZ (Public Health), financial matters were arranged by the Township, and at the start of the AWBZ, they had to transfer the funds from the residents. It was then put on their own account.

In one way or another, the city of Utrecht has, however, forgot to arrange for Mr. Jacob, but suddenly; they came with it for the day. As it turns out, he saved a small fortune for the military service he did in the First World War.

The first thing I did was ask Mr. Grondman to buy the best watch for him. The joy of Mr. Jacob was indescribable; tears ran down his cheeks.

But the most tragic was that Mr. Jacob was married before entering the military. His wife, all these years, lived in poverty. A candy shop had been her salvation, but she has had a bitter life. She had always been alone and only recently deceased.

How the City of Utrecht was able to pull this off is still a mystery to me.

Until the death of Mr. Meijer, we were good to him. Mr. Grondman bought him new clothes and shoes. The man was glad that he could finally put away that grubby raincoat.

Tragic is an understatement.

*

There were many things that seems regular, but also a tragic comic:

One day there was fierce ring and a confused man shouted, "*I hit him, but I do not see him.*" With Physician Director Hoekstra in his flowing white coat in front, we rushed to the Naarderstraat and indeed we saw no one injured. Suddenly, there was a cry. He was found sticking out of the big beech next to Naarderstraat. He was just launched and he got there. Luckily, he was not hurt too much.

On the very day that the elevator was broken a resident on the top floor set his curtains on fire accidentally because of his cigar. Fortunately we were able to extinguish it quickly, but the water ran out of the ceiling of the office.

Still, I like hearing a Psalm or Song. I think of those people who went to the weekly church service; that was really coming home for them.

Attracting the first student aides in the West Indies. They were so loud that I had to stand to speak. They did freezing in the Netherlands. They blow the heating away!

So I could go on, but what is more important is that there are always boys and girls who are attracted to the care of others.

Hats off!

SWEET MEMORIES

I immediately pulled to a stop. There was a Jeep DAF 66 YA along the Naarderstraat of Laren!

You would expect a big Land Rover or a BMW, but no. It was a simple jeep that was only used to manufacture goods.

Many, so many years I had ridden one of those through the province from my job as a hospital director in Bilthoven. When they saw that jeep, they knew that I was there.

Because my wife, who was passed away, was disabled, we always drove a DAF or later an automatic Volvo.

It was a fantastic invention that can still be found in several other car brands, but the original version is no longer made.

I had a column-plate fastened by the emblem of the hospital. I regularly visit the boys at the Asthma Center. I would knock and ask, "Mr. Prins, is the jeep is yours?"

I would take them immediately for a ride. I just knew how they felt for being asthmatic.

My secretary saw it. She just shook his head and thought that I had become a child, but it was still great!

All kinds of memories competed for primacy:

- The rides with fellows who got scared while I smoke a cigar with my loose hands.

- The children's parties, where enthusiastic boys were all over the jeep.

- The fire in engine that was barely extinguished.

- The icicles hanging from the roof as I drove to the hospital.

- That time I drove in a tuxedo and a cigar on my head around the village.

- Never had to wear a seat belt; it was not required, according to the registration.

- All those times that I had other cars became a drag, because I wasn't used to them.

- That time I did not notice a peacock from the hospital came home with me on my jeep. I only saw it climbing out of the jeep when I was seated at the table to eat.

It always required a lot of maintenance. Luckily, I had a spare starter that I could put in there in no time. It frequently had to be welded, have the holes filled, painted, and so on.

Finally, the car was over 25 years old and was considered as an antique car free from road tax.

There was a time when I have seen people jumped to attention and saluted on a toll gate. I needed no ticket!

I could not believe it. It happened twice and the second time still felt incredible.

After twenty years, I have finally decided to part with the jeep by selling it to a lover. I do regret doing that.

THE DAY AFTER

With a relieved mind, I looked over the beautiful green of our village in Laren. I was seated on the beautiful terrace of the Café het Bonte Paard and sipping a beer.

Young mothers drove fearlessly with their children.

Girls were all chatting about the zebras while on their way to their beloved terrace to enjoy a glass of prosecco.

Cars and trucks already inhabited the crossroads.

I had seen it all once, but today I had a different feeling; a sense of relief.

Because it has been barely 24 hours since I was on the operating table, while the surgeon was busy repairing a triple fracture.

After that, he told me that it was very tiring, but they were able to repair everything.

It was quite a day. The operation was to be performed during daytime in Hospital of Tergooi in Hilversum.

At half past twelve, I was brought in the F2 department. I was laid in bed and prepared for surgery. Sometime later, I was taken to the operating room. The anesthetist and surgeon were introduced to me and they began to plan out the whole operation.

I had to wait again. There were seven people in the operating room. The only one missing was the anesthesiologist. A few men came looking for him. He came back panting.

Then I do not remember anything until I woke up and was very thirsty.

After two hours, I was able to go back to the daytime surgery department. I also spent two hours there. I was allowed to drink and eat a biscuit.

After seven more hours, I was allowed to go home. I was welcomed with relief.

I felt better than the last few years. It was just awesome!

But why am I telling you this fact? That's because I'm from the large amount of impressed faces that I have seen.

Because I am a retired hospital director, I was used to having to confront anything that had gone wrong. I just always believed that everything would go wrong. Even as a private individual I had unfortunately had the necessary experience. So I was expecting the worst when I was admitted.

Fortunately, there was nothing wrong and I came into a competent and most capable hands!

And so the next day, there I was, with a beer on a terrace, satisfied under the sun. So health care can also be great!

THE COMMUTER

A long time ago, I lived in Bussum and had to commute to Amsterdam for work. Twice a day, I was in the midst of a brooding, sweating, coughing, and smelly crowd in the train.

I often panic of thought of having to do it for the rest of my working life. I looked around and saw the sadness in everyone's faces.

My commuter days were pretty much the same with Mr. Rob Hoogland, the columnist who wrote that. I did have very special memories of it.

Bussum is a real commuter location. Every day, you see a stream of people with briefcases and suitcases rushing through the streets, on their way to Naarden - Bussum or P & R station in Bussum Zuid.

The former station had a special atmosphere. It was beautiful but also depressing at the same time. A continuous series of trains came to Amsterdam.

As a new commuter, marvel and wonder about what you are going through.

Memories of the stations:

- What particularly stuck is that stations in large cities are much like open systems.

- At 9:00, the whores are out.

- Mayonnaise dripping from the handrail of the escalator.

- Amstel, you will be welcomed by a group waiting for you; using drug dealers.

- The opera singer in the tunnel.

- The pigeon stroking through your hair.

- The blind man who is not helped, but is knocked over.

Memories of passengers:

- Opposing sides NS personal summit to discuss reorganization and stupid mayors in the train.

- Giggling girls with huge backpacks that whack you off the train.

- From the backpack of a man stuck a large bread knife. People were afraid of terrorism.

- The woman with her tackle and short skirt.

- The transparent Perspex case with an apple and brown bread.

- *"Friendly, Personable and Helpful" text* on a briefcase.

- Holidaymakers heading to Zandvoort with umbrellas and cooler.

- Summers with sullen-looking farmers in shorts. The wife and kids go to Zandvoort.

- The horde of women who were in the train worms, right after their visit to the Home Exhibition.

- Wanderer: *"Why would you work, look at me, I'm happy."* All commuters remain in their newspapers.

- The judge holding a stack of criminal records and files.

- A Commissioner of the Queen with a pipe in his mouth.

- The train to Maastricht always looked clean and filled with friendly people.

- A gentleman who drank half a bottle of red wine and a classy lady who was smoking a cigar.

- The train to Arnhem was always very old and dirty, filled with the outcast among the public. It was like a direct route to the prison in Arnhem. The people had to be pushed like in Japan.

*

Memories of trains:

- The train that ran away from The Hague.

- A waving flag of a stationary train

- *"A communication exclusively for Mr. X, the NS wishes Mr. X a wonderful meal, thank you"*

- *"Good evening, ladies and gentlemen, do you want to switch to the whistle of chairs?"*

- *"An urgent request to the passengers on the balconies not to come to the doors due to a defect."*

- *"Welcome to the ice cream shop",* called the conductor of a train with a broken heater.

- Mud on the benches and backrests.

*

Memories of advertising slogans:

- The train, a different view of the world.

- New: chat box on wheels.

- Maybe your fellow passenger thinks the same way about you.

- Mozart would also travel with a walkman.

- Looking in the mirror, admiring her quietly

- Nose picking.

- You are in a pasture, and the cattle appears.

- Where all the interesting people are.

*

Reminder of the Christmas season:

It's really time for a message to be precisely a Christmas message. It's that time again when we celebrate Christmas in our own way.

For some time we are under the influence of the Christmas spirit. Wherever we go, we hear Christmas music, pine scent imposes itself, we see twinkling lights, and the windows look inviting to us.

In the families the necessary requirements are expressed by everyone, and it is fortunate that many people receive a thirteenth month; otherwise it would be a sad thing.

I remember one Christmas; I had to work in Amsterdam for a nursing home for somatic and geriatric patients.

One of the duties of all employees was assisting with the Christmas celebrations of the residents.

That year it was my turn.

I was able to imagine anything, but it was still a nice place, the food looked neat, pleasant music, and all the residents were having fun.

For the employees, it was an unusual and heavy evening.

There were many people who could not eat, so they had to be fed. Other residents was taking too much time at the table too and had to be helped with other things.

It was with mixed feelings that I accepted the journey home.

At the Amstel station, I saw just the van of the Salvation Army starting off with a new batch of vagabonds from their boxes. They got themselves a temporary roof over their head. I was hoping that the orchestra of the Army does not play too much.

At the railway station, while waiting for my train, the TV was on and showed us the news.

In a remote corner of the world was a Christmas tree decorated with hand grenades; soldiers with drawn faces sang Silent Night O Holy Night.

Yeltsin stumbled again as a walking advertisement.

And Clinton? He looked heavenly when he lighted the big Christmas tree in Washington.

My train rattled into the station.

In the smoking compartment train, I saw my friend, a director of the Dutch Central Bank.

After we had learned our cigars, we exchanged our experiences. He once went to a very pleasant dinner for the top people of the financial world.

Many drinks, cigars, fine cuisine, and of course, an optimistic speech by the President of the Dutch Bank.

The ladies dressed in evening clothes that were revealing.

There was a lot of noise in the coupe and snow blew in

We thought it could not get worse, but the lights went out!

After some time, came in the light of a flashlight. A driver picked us up and took us to a compartment where the conductors are.

We parted in Weesp and wished each other good days. The last part of the trip were moments of contemplation, I looked back on the past year. The transition from old to new and promises for the future.

*

Memory of a Disaster:

That harmony and peace in the heart are not just reserved for the individual, but can include a lot more people. It is evident from the following that I experienced:

I worked in a large health center in Amsterdam, which was a melting pot of cultures and nationalities for several years.

The language was even English.

There, you could experience a real Amsterdam oldie being helped by an employee of African descent in an endearing manner; they did not understand each other, but they understood with each other needed well.

However, the work there has one drawback; you had to commute.

Commuting doesn't really sound like a nice thought, but it is possible to change your idea about it.

So I rode the usual train to Amsterdam the morning after the crash of a cargo plane on a large flat where hundreds where killed in the part of Amsterdam that is named Bijlmer.

The events of the previous evening were burned into my brain; the incredible mess, the scorching heat, the countless workers, and the seemingly endless series of ambulances.

There was also the panic of the residents, the fear, and the sadness, the incredible efforts of the workers, and the involvement of everyone.

When I got to the Bijlmer, it was quieter than it already was; the papers were filed, the laptops were dropped, and everyone looked deep in thought at the scene of the crime.

On the Amstel station, there was an oppressive silence.

There were no running footsteps, no shouting, no drug addicts, no snatchers, and no people in sleeping bags on the floor.

Yes, even the familiar smell of urine was gone. There was just total silence.

In that silence, you just felt an oneness with each other that was previously unthinkable.

Behind the Amstel station is the headquarters of the Hells Angels, in the shadow of the Bijlmer prison. It was surrounded by shady businesses.

The Hells Angels had hung the flag of the Netherlands at half-mast. I stood there for a long time, looking at the many symbols of togetherness.

When I traveled by train to go home that night, I saw in the east, against an inky sky, the platforms with people busy with their macabre work.

In the West, I saw the sun setting in the clear evening sky.

The Sun is the symbol of light and life; the life that went on, but never more so than before.

On that night, I saw the light and experienced Harmony in my heart and environment.

This experience gives me the conviction that we will all agree to go together and work in a different constellation as before.

*

FINALLY:

A study on my work showed that employees who lived more than twenty miles away, in eighty percent of the cases, do not remain longer than a year in service.

Even the commuters who are optimists could not stay longer.

After a few years, I gave it up. It was dulling and numbing at the same time, but I look back gratefully.

The commuters gave me an insight on life and the people in that life.

The sadness of human existence is there because there seemed to no moving forward between those rails.

But on the other side, it gives surprising insights; and I would have not wanted to miss that.

SUNDAY`S REST

What a quiet Sunday, it seemed to be, but it was cruelly disturbed by the continuing roar of fire sirens.

Awakened from a dreamless sleep, we looked at each other and wondered whether the arsonist had struck again; are cars on fire again? If so, is it in Laren? Blaricum? Or the houses again?

The fire engines drove back and forth. We soon found out that it was the house on the border of Laren and Blaricum. It was already the second time that there was a fire on that place!

Many came to assist in the area; even Nederhorst den Berg came to rescue. There was a handful of work.

In the afternoon, I was sitting with a cup of tea when the silence broke with the violent sounds of the sirens. This time, there were three motorcycle cops who passed by our house in a flash. They followed by three loud police cars.

What the hell was going? We have also heard the police helicopter coming. It remained above the Mauve Heather.

Was John de Mol kidnapped or Linda? Or Gordon was quarreling with the members of his Voices? Everything is just possible in the Gooi!

It turned out that there was a protest in Torenlaan in Blaricum. People were forced to leave their houses over a financial dispute settlement. The police were summoned; beaten people, put them in chains, and thrown them in a prison in Hilversum.

The evening was uneventful until the time we wanted to go to bed. It seemed like hell really broke.

Sirens just went on and on. There was chaos and there seemed to be no end of it.

Slowly, the sky above Laren turned red. It became clear that there was something seriously wrong. It was not just a small car fire.

The sawmill of Van Dijk was on fire, along with the businesses located on the premises. The fire had reached the library and was fully enforced to ashes.

The fire immediately swallowed 20 cars on the spot, but they managed to prevent the fire from spreading to the many thatched houses in the center of Laren with great difficulty.

Even fire trucks came from Amersfoort to help.

Local residents did their best to save their valuables. The horses were taken away and the chickens flew into the trees. During the night, they were caught in the Town Hall and later placed with their families or a Motel in the Witte Bergen.

At four in the morning, the fire was under control, but the entire village remained closed on Monday. Authorities were busy investigating the cause of the fire.

Initially, a 15-year-old boy was arrested, but after a few days, he proved his innocence.

From examination of the residents, it appeared that the fire started in several spots. It was definitely an indicated arson.

They had advanced plans to build apartments in this area; this development has now emerged clearly in gear.

Thus the long-troubled day came to an end.

GRAVE FLOWERS

In our lives, we are faced with all sorts of things, such as joy and sorrow; life and death.

These contradictions are inseparable. To live without different sides would not let us experience real joy and happiness.

In every city, there is a quiet and secluded place.

There are many places like that in the Gooi. Mostly places by religious groups: Catholic, Old Catholic, Protestant, Reformed, Jewish, and the rest on the General Cemetery.

There is a unique place in the Gooi region on the border of Blaricum where the General Cemetery is located. There is a "mountain" located on the site with also a camping. It is where joy mixes up with sorrow.

This cemetery's absolute tranquility reigns. It is located right next to a unique botanical garden.

The tombs are perfectly maintained. Many people make use of the opportunity to enjoy the beautiful woods whenever they visit.

It reminds me of a cemetery elsewhere in the country where I learned a lot since my first wife has found her resting place there.

During one of those visits, I noticed that there are a lot of men with pruning and hedge trimmers. So I looked at the four men consecutively and dutifully seeking their way toward the grave of their deceased life partners.

But at the same time, I noticed that there were several women who claim men torn by grief with an excuse. They were able to carry a conversation about their often empty and quiet life after the death of their partner. Were these women attempting to just chat or entice those men? You would wonder about it too.

It even went crazier when I read in the newspaper about the tomb of the famous Irish writer, Oscar Wilde, in Paris on Père Lachaise. There is a thick glass for his tombstone.

This man appears to have been the man who was loved by hundreds of women. He was a great charmer

There had been so many women who visited this tomb and lipstick marks were left all over his tombstone. It became damaged so they put a protective glass plate to preserve the whole thing.

On the glass plate were plenty of crimson traces of lips that had touched him.

What a "hunk", that man must have been. 111 years after his death, there are still so many women out there who visited his grave and then kiss it.

Imagine how it had been before he died. He probably was not able to peacefully walk down the street.

Women bring a lot of joy in this life, but they can still support us even after our death.

THE ULTIMATE CHRISTMAS FEELING

"I Do" on the Laren Brink

Published, Region | December 13, 2011 | Source: Laarder Courant de Bel.

LAREN - A marriage was solemnized for the first time last Monday in the skating rink on Brink. Celine and Nick from Laren pulled off a fairytale-like wedding. The guests skated on rink after the ceremony.

A handful of people watched the ceremony from behind the fence. Antoinette van de Brink, president of the Laren Historical, gave blessings to the couple, but the official part was done by an official of the Civil Registry. The arrival of the bride was very surprising. She was in a sleigh with a real reindeer from Lapland. The mayor had given permission for this special moment.

*

We thought we had seen it all in Laren, but no, the couple added a very special and original chapter to the unforgettable happenings on Brink in Laren.

Further comment is superfluous: this is really how the ultimate Christmas spirit feels like.

We wish the couple all the best!

GO ON

We write now in **the year 2020.** Much has remained the same in Laren. We still see the neatly trimmed hedges, old farmhouses and beautiful fields. On the ecological market, still plays the Ukrainian orchestra and a lot of people still drive expensive cars.

At the Gas Pump, you would see Ferraris and Bentley's, all washed and polished. The fashion stores still do good business and it's still a pleasure to walk through it.

Yet the differences are:

There is a woman who brings papers in a Mercedes S 500. It was impossible back then. Are women more useful now? Are they able to finally take care of their own income? Or they are still a result of credit crisis? We do not really know, but it makes you wonder.

In a beautiful thatched house, four gloomy-looking men are playing cards on a table covered with green cloth. It seems they are bored and unemployed.

The Café Het Bonte Paard, a man is sulking about the upcoming Christmas. When asked what he will do with that gloomy Christmas he answers *"I will go to see the parent-in-laws of my daughter, and I'm not happy about it. They all sing terrible Christmas carols, and they'd just make me want a drink."*

*

Laren was an oasis in the Netherlands. It is now clear that the variegation of the Netherlands has now reached Laren.

Some years ago, the first signs can already be seen at the **College De Brink**, and now, it is ubiquitous.

Everyone is remarkably dealing with each other in a harmonious way. There seems to problems unlike before.

On inquiry, it appears that it is no coincidence that there is a clear municipal policy back in the form of an Integration officer who had been appointed. His name is Ahmed.

Yes, yes, the same one we saw as the homeless vendor and also the one that appeared in the Society Jan Hamdorff.

It turned out to have been a golden opportunity for him. It is a great insight into human nature and his communication skills made him well and easily dealt with all the population.

His insights for being an Imam and a former mayor in Iran made him more efficient for the job.

His meeting in the societies with the Mayor of Laren to fulfill this function was very much anticipated.

It had been a success, all these years.

*

The Laarder Call, the local newspaper, was on the bus with an attention-grabbing headline: SELECT OR PARTS.

It turned out that mayoral elections were to be organized; completely contrary to expectations that were now required by law in the Netherlands.

The current mayor had set course for re-election. But the new local party "Laren Allen" suggested a quite surprising candidate; the Integration officer, Ahmed.

A dilemma presented itself, as both were very popular and immensely popular.

Rallies were organized, as well as debates.

But as time progressed, no one really knew who they are to vote. They discovered that both have no differences when it comes to personality.

*

The two candidates met at the **Pancake House ("The Coeswaerde")** for a meeting.

Seated with a farmer pancake for themselves, they started talking and came to the hopelessness of the situation.

They discovered that they could get along fine. They had drinks; only a cup of strong coffee for they still had to discuss matters.

And then the penny dropped.

Together, they walked across the street to the **Warrekam** for the next election meeting.

They came on stage and then did the proposal to the office of mayor and the integration work together as a duo.

They wanted to work together and fill their duties that way to optimize their services.

The people took them on the shoulder and they did it!

LONELY AFTER CHRISTMAS

After an extensive Christmas breakfast, it was time for a refreshing walk in preparation for the approaching dinner. It was a green Christmas this year, but keep in mind that it was winter. Like other years, it was noticed that there are so many vacant homes, especially the larger houses, country houses, bungalows etc. The view of the winter was really nice.

This was in stark contrast to the older lady, who even to this day, was the office of the dental technician across the street from our house. She spends her whole time to clean! Every Sunday, she dutifully cleans her old bike for hours. She was able to support herself and perhaps even buy her grandchild something because of her retirement.

The contrasts are everywhere, but here in the luxurious the Gooi, homeless people still huddled in the middle of Laren.

It reminded me of an encounter I had in central London. A homeless person sitting on the ground raised a plastic cup at me with a questioning and pleading look in his eyes. Of course I did what any decent person did. I gave him a few Euros in the cup and stopped at the same time. There was a small dog and it licked my hand gratefully. Moments later, I looked at the man again and saw a strange light shining from his eyes. Was it a meeting with THE LIGHT?

But back to today, the preparations for Christmas dinner restaurants affected a lot of employees. They were ready to receive the necessary guests that day and give them what they asked, while their partners were alone with their children at the Christmas table, but they had little choice in this society.

This Christmas Eve we ate at the famous restaurant "De Vrije Heren" in Laren. The walk towards the place was lighted by Christmas lights on the trees. There were children doing their laps on the skating rink. It looked nice from the restaurant, which is filled by Christmas decorations. Everything was just beautiful to see. The place was busy, but we enjoyed everything that was served to us.

Things got busier as the evening approached, especially in the cafés. It became so busy that we asked the waiter for the reason of it. He told me that those were people who did not know each other physically, but had found each other on Facebook.

They were all single or divorced people escaping the loneliness of Christmas.

Well, it was a success! It was incredible to see how strangers soon became comfortable with each other.

Their enthusiasm and joy swept through the establishment. The musicians played even more excited than before. The dance floor was always crowded, but this time, it was not!
154

Next to us was a couple that was initially very similar to each other, but in the course of the evening, their attention was increasingly drawn to the events in the café. Occasionally, the guests arrived at the different tables talking to each other, and at one point a regular table next to us was set up in an artistic way.

To our amazement, the man sank down on one knee and spoke to the lady. He asked her to marry him. Everything stopped and everyone watched in amazement. Hesitantly, the lady stood and hugged her man. She turned him down!

She walked out of the place and I wondered how things would be now for the two of them, but one thing is for certain; they left everyone behind in silence. No one knew what to do next.

The man was so alone and did not know where to look. It's crazy how he was just holding hands with his partner a few minutes ago, and now he is all alone.

LONELY AFTER CHRISTMAS

A NEW SPRING

It was March 30 and spring officially begins in Laren!

This is evident from everything:

Friday, March 30, at 5 pm: Councilor de Jong made it to the grand opening of the Brink Project.

He came to honor the place.

From September last year, a major renovation of the street around Brink took place with the primary aim to create a safer place for the cycling citizens.

The shopkeepers' complained about the whole thing.

But the past three months was a real pinnacle. The Brink was completely closed to the traffic! A surreal image was a result.

Vehicles had to drive around Brink and there were serious traffic problems.

Laren had also become unreachable.

Fortunately, some organizations helped with the whole situation so eased up a little.

The local people of Laren still had a hard time making their way through the streets. They all had a hard time with looking for passable roads in the area. Everyone expressed genuine anger for motorists who made traffic like a living hell.

But now, here comes the opening ceremony. Everything was done thanks to the great efforts of the contractor and his employees. They worked really hard and non-stop, so now was their time to celebrate!

It's all been wonderful for the village. The streets and sidewalks look wonderful.

It will not be long until the normal life regains its course, and the memory of this difficult period fades.

That period being behind us is particularly evident from the fact that the bars and restaurants are full again. The white-coated waiters do their best to process all orders.

Laren: the village where a glass of white wine is more expensive than a serving of pancakes!

The first Maserati coupe is already signaled again with blond beauties behind the wheel. You see women everywhere looking for bargains.

The trees run out and the grass springs out of the ground.

So after a long and harsh winter, it is a pleasure to be able to go back on the road and enjoy the beautiful weather. Everyone went on with their businesses.

Today, Sunday, April 1, I was sitting on the terrace enjoying the nice village.

The village is overrun by tourists and shoppers; an unusual combination.

There are several streams of people on their way to the Basilica to attend the Palm Sunday.

The music of street musicians echo throughout the streets; the violin sounded a bit false but that does not matter.

It promises to be a great year!

SOURCES

Thank you for the information and photos on the following sources:

- All the mentioned newspapers like the Gooi en Eemlander, de Pers, Vrij Nederland, De Telegraaf, RTV NH, de Bel and HDC Media

- Wikipedia, the free encyclopedia
  http://nl.wikipedia.org/wiki/Hoofdpagina

- http://www.historielaren.nl

- http://www.album.zoom.nl

- http://www.larenseshoppingmall.nl

- http://www.mauve.nl

- Website of the Municipality Laren http://www.laren.nl

- Website Gooi Nature http://www.gnr.nl

- http://www.vuursche.nl

- http://www.ijsopdebrink.nl

- http://www.uitgeverijvanwijland.nl

- http://www.devalk.com/kunstenaars

- http://www.singerlaren.nl

- http://www.larensbehoud.nl

- http://www.larenjazz.nl

- http://www.vivium.nl

- http://www.rtl.nl/soaps/gooischevrouwen

- http://www.rtl.nl/reality/gooischemeisjes

- http://www.belkerken.nl/sintjan/processie

- http://www.hamdorffetenendrinken.nl

- http://www.devalk.com/kunstenaars/hamdorff/hamdorff.html

- http:/ / www.historielaren.nl

- http://www.laardercourant.nl

- http://www.oogoplaren.nl

And all other sources.

ABOUT THE AUTHOR

In the course of his life as a Director in the Healthcare Economist, Jan Prins (1946) always found great pleasure in writing policy papers in a way that it was clear to everyone in the organization. His pleasure in writing also extended in a variety of other administrative activities and consultancy. In writing books, he has embarked on a new path. There are more than ten of his books published, including the well-known book "The Gooi".

OTHER WORK OF JAN PRINS

Denkend aan Boekhouders

Pensionado

Wie was Arm en wie was Rijk?

Reizen om te Rijzen

Eva

De Denker Vertelt

Bestemming Bereikt

Vrij Worden

Gooi-land

De Leestafel

Strepen

More information on: www.janprins.com

www.ingramcontent.com/pod-product-compliance
Lightning Source LLC
Chambersburg PA
CBHW060310290526
45789CB00001B/469